J12

DRESSAGE MASTERCLASS

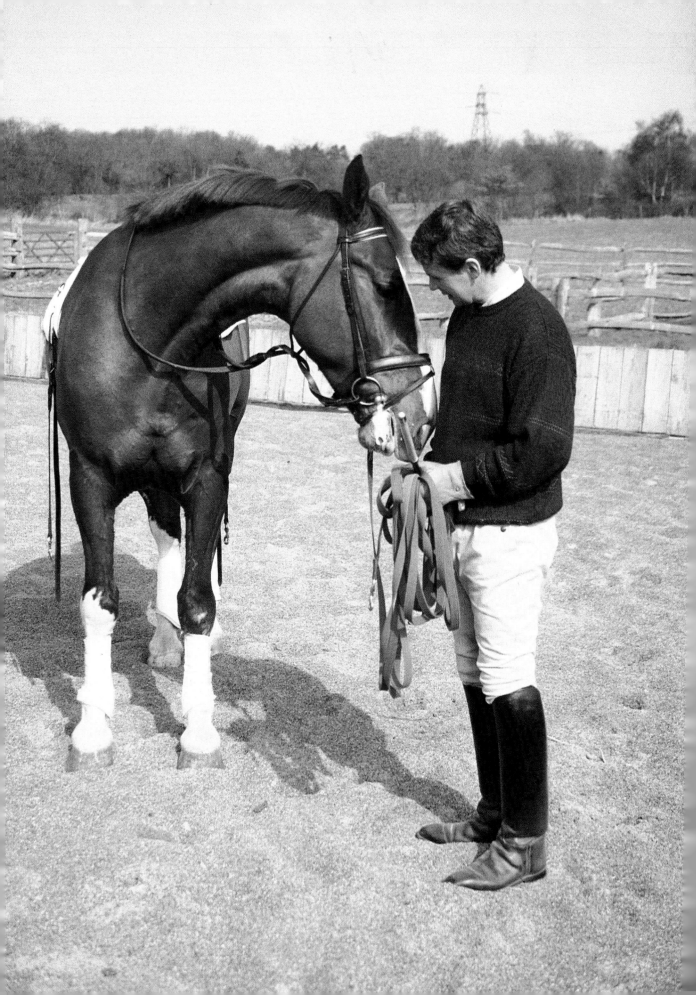

DRESSAGE MASTERCLASS

·with Dane Rawlins

KAREN RYECART

David & Charles

*To my father, Derek; my wife, Maureen; and
my children, Daniel and Anne-Marie*

*Schooling photographs by Karen Ryecart;
photographs on pp8–23, 122 and 126 by Kit Houghton;
all other photographs from Dane Rawlins' personal
 collection*

Line illustrations by Elaine Campling

A DAVID & CHARLES BOOK

Copyright © Karen Ryecart and Dane Rawlins 1995
First published 1995

Karen Ryecart and Dane Rawlins have asserted their right to
be identified as authors of this work in accordance with the
Copyright, Designs and Patents Act 1988.

A catalogue record for this book is available from the
British Library.

ISBN 0 7153 0269 8

Printed in England by BPC Paulton Books Ltd
for David & Charles
Brunel House   Newton Abbot   Devon

CONTENTS

Preface 7

1 Establishing the Partnership 24

2 Lungeing and Long Reining 30
  • *Problem Solver* 44

3 Riding Circles, Straight Lines and Transitions 50
  • *Problem Solver* 62

4 Advancing Self-carriage 66
  • *Problem Solver* 76

5 Developing Flexibility:
  Introducing Extensions and Lateral Work 77
  • *Problem Solver* 98

6 The Flying Change 102
  • *Problem Solver* 110

7 Pirouettes, Piaffe and Passage 118
  • *Problem Solver* 133

8 The Test: Preparing for the Competition
  and Riding the Test 136
  • *A Typical Novice Test* 144

Index 149

Acknowledgements 152

PREFACE

The reason for my involvement in this wonderful way of life is **The Horse**. He demands from me the whole range of emotions that can possibly exist: from the extremes of frustration when I fail, to the heights of ecstasy when I succeed, he reminds me that it is not me, but *we*. It is therefore a *partnership* that I am trying to build when I train, whether it is between myself and my horse or between my students and their mounts. Riding for me has to be a matter of both horse and rider together attempting to resolve the problems and difficulties that arise, and not the rider pitching himself against the horse. Its whole purpose is the formation of a partnership which should be based on mutual respect and trust, which in turn should lead to a real and lasting friendship.

Perhaps this is a rather idealised vision, but nonetheless it is a goal that should be strived for, and a goal that will take time to become reality. If there is one thing that a rider should repeat to himself again and again, it is the phrase 'I have time'. This is not to say that time should be wasted or that a recalcitrant horse should be allowed to get away with anything, but it does take time to teach and train any animal. The fact that the horse has a marvellous memory can work in our favour, its only disadvantage being that he will remember the bad as well as the good. We must therefore make sure that we maximise the input of good ideas to his brain and minimise anything else. The brain has been compared to a computer, but it doesn't have the same erase button; therefore what goes in sometimes stays in for good, but it may not always be what we want him to retain.

What are we trying to achieve by training the horse? The answer is, I believe, that the trainer is trying to create from a basically raw if not wild animal, one that is to a certain extent tamed and domesticated. In the case of the horse, we are taking an animal that if left alone in its natural surroundings would graze almost continuously from whatever vegetation was afforded to it from its environment. It would defend itself from any danger, real or imagined, by fight or by flight. And those who have seen a horse really fight would soon lose any sweet ideas they might have had of it being a pleasant-natured, docile creature. Horses use all four hooves and teeth, together with amazing agility, to disable and even kill their opponents. They can also spin away and flee, again a feat performed with incredible speed and dexterity by even the most dull-looking of beasts. I am pointing this out not to scare you, but to draw your attention to the true nature of the animal that we are hoping to educate.

For most people nowadays even the youngest of horses have been handled from birth. They are accustomed to man, and for the most part they will tolerate if not accept his presence. What the trainer has to achieve will involve him making use of all the horse's senses, his ability to see, feel, hear and even in a more limited sense, to smell; only in this way will we have a chance to build up a true partnership with the horse.

Left: Daphne Edwards-Haagmans (Can) on Voodoo, preparing for a competition

Previous page: Lizzie Loriston-Clarke (GB) shows a good beginning to a circle during the national medium championships at Goodwood

Overleaf: Charlotte Bredahl with Monsieur (USA). Although the horse is a little short in the neck, he is showing plenty of expression in this extended trot

*Above: A very enthusiastic aid from Doris Ramsier (Sui)
on Renatus during the medium canter flying change*

Left: A picture of harmony in extended trot

Right: Markus Tecklenborg on Franklin (FRG) shows how a horse should 'sit' in the canter pirouette

Overleaf: Lizzie Loriston-Clarke (GB) shows a super collected canter through the corner on Spiderman at Goodwood 1992

Above: Tineke Bartels (Hol) and Olympic Courage in passage; an impressive picture of one of my favourite horses

Right: This horse looks in the peak of fitness at the Seoul Olympics. It's hard to believe he was over twenty years old! Anne-Marie Sanders-Keyzer (Hol) on Amon

Left: A good advertisement for dressage: Lizzie Loriston-Clarke (GB) during the prize-giving display at Royal Windsor

Above: Dressage in another form: carriage driver Alwyn Holder and his team of cobs perform their dressage test at an international event

ESTABLISHING THE PARTNERSHIP

Assuming that to start with the horse is relatively untrained, it is most important that the trainer uses his senses of feel and touch to influence the horse at first; initially to dominate him to a certain extent, but as training proceeds it is far more important that he is trained in such a way as to encourage him to want to do what you ask of him. This requires a degree of willingness in the horse's nature, which may not initially be present. Obviously some horses are more submissive than others, but most horses will put up some resistance to a rider's requests since these may at first seem alien to their natural way of going.

The rider can influence the horse considerably by way of its basic senses: these are primarily vision, feel and hearing, and to a lesser extent its sense of smell. Horses obviously have a very acute sense of hearing, and may react to any noise; a simple example is that of a foal taking fright as his stable door is opened. This must therefore always be kept in mind in the handling and training of the horse, and as trainer, you should always do your best to apply to the horse's senses in a calm and gentle way. This may be by modifying your voice to a soothing tone on approach, or by stretching out your hand so the horse has the opportunity to touch you before you make contact with him.

This simple approach has been used for many years by all horsemasters as a method of encouraging the horse to respond. He must be able to hear, feel and see you all the time until his confidence reaches a level where he becomes more inquisitive about than frightened by your presence. It is important to establish these qualities in a horse when he is still a foal, so that later they can be developed to a higher degree throughout the horse's training. The stable is the place of training at first: the horse should be trained to move over if you push him, in an orderly fashion and in prompt response to your request; he should not push you back or be in any way your boss. Similarly, if you ask him to pick up his foot, you expect him to pick it up, when and how you ask.

It is therefore very important to make an impression on the horse in the stable. In demanding the immediacy of his reaction, you should not however make the horse in any way fearful of you; merely responsive to your requests. It is important, too, that you are handling a horse that you really like. Inevitably you will come across horses that you don't get on with, and with these you may be less tempered in your approach: in this sort of situation it is therefore wiser to leave their training to someone who can actually strike up a rapport with them. Your horse must be looked upon as your friend, and only in this way can basic trust and understanding be built up between you. The partnership may not be immediately apparent, but can be developed by spending time in the stable getting to know your horse, before actually commencing the ridden work.

Any tension in the horse needs to be transformed to an alert form of relaxation, so that he is responsive and reactive, but without his nature of performance being marred by this tension. Again, it is important that the horse actually wants to do what you ask of him, rather than doing it because you are in such a position as to dominate him. It is when this stage is reached that you can actually claim to have trained the horse rather than to have merely dominated him through the use of iron will. This is a point that I will reiterate throughout this book because it is so important: that when the horse has been taught he has genuinely *learned*, rather than having been forced against his will to do what was required of him.

Sometimes it's nice to relax after work; here Hopscotch plays 'follow my leader'!

Most people tend to get horses when they are older than a foal, normally in their third or fourth year, or sometimes even older. Nonetheless, the same basic principles apply as those established here: always make use of the visual, tactile and auditory aids at whatever level you take on the training of a horse whether you are establishing these basics in a foal, or reapplying them to the older horse. Therefore the fundamental principles of training must first be established in the stable in order to avoid problems later in the ridden training of the horse.

All horses will undoubtedly respond to the various stimuli discussed here, but their responses are bound to be different in nature. The sharper and more nervous horse will need gentle, understanding handling, and may take more time to respond positively to your efforts than the less perceptive horse. Just as when a fly lands on a horse's back and it responds in a certain way to this stimulus, so too do different horses respond to you – for example, when you touch them lightly in the stable as a signal for them to move over; some may rush over to one side, whilst others may push you back. Our job as trainer of the horse is therefore to educate him to become responsive in his actions, to the extent that his responses are neither too sharp

nor too lax, so that all further training can be continued with the maximum of ease.

Taking his training one step further, the horse will have to learn to walk along beside you, and to accept being bridled. He must learn to walk at the pace you wish him to go at, and offer no resistance to the bridle. Initially avoid situations in which you may lose control, and try to be in the best possible position to influence the horse. This may mean that at first you have to go along to a certain extent with the horse's requirements; so if he wants to go in one direction, then move quietly with him, avoiding all possible confrontations, until he learns to walk with you. As he learns to trust you, he can then gradually be taught to walk in the direction that you want him to go.

The basic training should be started in the stable, where the horse can be walked around gently in small circles, without the likelihood of the handler losing control. Later, progress into the paddock or school. Make sure that you lead the horse with a long enough line, so that if he is flighty to start with, you can stand back and let him learn to cope with the situation himself before you start to

influence him. I have a theory that you can't actually make a horse listen until he is ready to listen to you. So, for example, when you first bring the horse out of the stable and he is a little flighty, you really only have limited control over his actions until he settles down and is ready to co-operate with you.

It must be remembered that there is no way we can physically dominate the horse, who may weigh up to seven hundred kilos (1500lb), compared to an average human weight of ninety kilos (190lb). The only part of his anatomy which we can attempt to control is his brain: he therefore has to be convinced that the handler is in control, and so learns to trust and obey him. Gradually the level of control can be built up, and developed into that special relationship between horse and owner that we would all ideally like to achieve. Sheer physical strength is therefore not the solution to the barriers that the horse will inevitably put up throughout all the stages in his training. It may be of use at times, but in the long run it will be more of a hindrance than a help.

Many of the problems involved with correcting a horse are not directly concerned with telling him not to do something, but rather with refocusing him so that his attention is centred mostly on you, and not on external factors which may influence him. A simple example of this may be if you were in the stable with a horse which saw something over the door, or out of the window, and was startled at it. This would be the kind of situation when the horse may jump on your foot, or push you out of the way in his fright, but it is no use trying to seek some kind of retribution against him for doing this. By all means give him a good slap on the shoulder to let him know you are there, but don't make the mistake of thinking that you can punish him for doing it and get a response. All that can be done, as discussed, is to try and refocus his attention on to you, so that he is more attentive to what you are asking of him than of the initial factor that frightened him.

As horses get older they hopefully lose their tendency to be distracted, possibly because they become more accustomed to certain sights and sounds, but also because they focus more and more on their rider. In addition, the horse will have learned that the rider will not ask him to do anything that will cause him discomfort or pain, and so a trusting relationship will have built up between horse and rider. The horse will therefore offer less defence to anything he is asked to do, as he might have done when he was younger, and perhaps be confused by what was being asked of him. Confusion and tension are two of the greatest enemies that could be encountered when training a horse; confusion perhaps being the greater of the two evils, as this in turn may lead to tension. As trainers we must therefore make sure that all the aids and commands we give the horse are crystal clear in order to avoid misunderstandings and to progress effectively with his education.

In summary, we must be very clear and concise about what we ask the horse to do, so that any confusion or fear on his part is removed, making him happy to co-operate. When asked to react he should do so readily, with the minimum possible effort being made on our part to gain a response from him, so that the simple tasks of picking up his foot in the stable, or asking him to move over, really should be simple, with the horse responding willingly.

(Left) Horsted Bright Spark, a winner at International Goodwood, and who has put several young riders on the British team

'Bribery and corruption'

'Give the judge fifty quid and tell him I'll be on in a minute!'

It is always wise to remember that horses are potentially extremely dangerous, and whilst few are deliberately malicious, it is still possible to get hurt if you happen to be in the wrong place at the wrong time. You therefore have to be very aware of what is happening round about, and you have to make the horse aware of your presence, by influencing his senses of sight, hearing and feel, so that he knows where you are, and what you are going to do, and so that he respects you enough to comply with what you ask of him. He will then eventually begin to accept you as a normal presence in his environment, rather than someone or something that he should be wary of. Once this is achieved, that elusive feeling of partnership will start to build up, and ultimately you will hopefully reach the stage where instead of working against the horse's problems, you and the horse can work against them together, so that in the end it is you and him against the world, so to speak. If you manage to achieve this relationship with your

horse before you even begin to start tacking him up, or riding him, you will already have achieved many of the vital requirements that are needed to train your horse to a higher level.

I do believe in offering my horses titbits, because this can often help in building up the relationships, making the horse less afraid and more inclined to approach you. When he does something right that you have asked of him, it is good to reward him with a pat, a kind word, and a piece of sugar, because in this way he will learn it is good to co-operate. Obviously it is unwise to over-reward the horse in the way of titbits, as he may become pushy and demanding for more. However, if given sparingly and wisely, they can really help in training.

In addition, one must never underestimate the usefulness of the voice; it is one of the best aids we are equipped with to influence the horse. Used as a calming influence or as a reprimand, the horse can tell instantly from its intonation what is expected of him. When he knows his trainer well he will recognise him instantly, not only from his voice but even from his footfalls on the stable yard. Thus on its own, and certainly in conjunction with other aids, the voice is of immense help to any would-be trainer. The nervous horse can often be calmed, whilst the recalcitrant beast can be brought into line. I'm sure that many horsemen would tell you that a kind word, or even possibly a sharp comment, has got them out of what could have been a potentially serious situation. For example, when your horse has learned to stand still in the stable upon command by your voice, this may be used in a situation such as when he gets loose: the same command can be used to stop him, giving you the chance to pick up the reins and regain control.

Once you reach the stage with your horse that he accepts the saddle and bridle, one of the most useful things I find is to be able to move him around both inside and outside the stable, before actually putting a rider on him. For example, hold his bridle in your left hand, and with your right hand quietly push his ribcage away from you, which will cause him to step across and sideways with the right hind leg; then the exercise can be repeated on the other rein. By using these exercises, the horse will get used to being turned whilst having a contact on his mouth. Another thing you can do is just lead him forwards a couple of strides, and then push him a few strides back, keeping the contact with the hand. Once the horse gets used to this, it will make him much more responsible when it comes to asking him to move away from your leg in the ridden work.

All that has been discussed in this chapter really comes down to one thing: it is starting to teach the horse to accept the *aids*. The aids are the means by which we educate the horse to do our bidding. Many greater horsemen than I have written wonderful treatises on the aids, and all, with few exceptions, state that the aids applied should be gentle and soft, nothing more than a caress on the horse's side with the leg or hand, and so on. However, as far as I can see, very few go beyond this rather idealised instruction – according to some, one apparently need only touch the horse in such gentle fashion and he will do your bidding as if by magic, including training himself up to Grand Prix standard and winning the next available Olympic gold medal! Wonderful as this might be, not only would it require every horse in the world to be a saint, it would also have to be able to read and probably to have the power of speech, too.

On the other hand is the rider who relies mainly on his own physical strength, and hardly uses his rational thinking faculty at all. In my experience this has led to much confusion between horse and rider, particularly when we are talking about the everyday rider who has limited access to good training, or none at all.

The horse is actually a great gift to us, and whilst having every right to train and use him, we have no right whatsoever to abuse him. The one thing that must always be kept in mind with a dressage horse, as opposed to a show-jumping horse, is that whilst you can't *make* a jumping horse go over a large fence again and again, you can to a certain extent make a dressage horse do a piaffe or a half-pass repeatedly; as riders we must therefore be very aware that we do not overstep the mark. Each time you ride the horse, try to feel that you are educating him, no matter how advanced he may be, and don't push him to the point of fatigue whereby he won't learn any more, as this will be a waste of time. It is in this respect that dressage is such a wonderful discipline, because as well as us teaching the horse, he probably teaches us more than we will ever know.

A picture of harmony: the British Young Riders Dressage Scheme quadrille display team at the Mitsubishi Motors Badminton Horse Trials in 1995, trained and choreographed by Jennie Loriston-Clarke and Dane

2

LUNGEING AND LONG REINING

Lungeing and long reining are two extremely useful exercises in the early stages of training a horse, before he is ridden; they are almost equally as important in his further training, too, when the horse is more advanced. The purpose of both lungeing and long reining is to create a horse with an improved way of going that will make it easier for you to ride him.

However, before starting with any training it is important to have a clear view of what you are trying to achieve. The aim of dressage is to establish a physical and mental balance with the horse. This requires that his mental as well as his physical development are improved in a harmonious way, so that he gains in confidence as he becomes loose and supple; then he can offer willingly the work that the rider asks of him.

In the **walk** the horse should march freely forwards in a clear four-time beat. The walk may be performed at medium in collection, and in extension.

The **trot** is a two-time movement in which the legs move freely forwards in diagonal pairs, alternately and separated by a moment of suspension. The trot needs to be elastic and regular with good engagement of the hindquarters. The trot may be performed at medium, in collection, and in extension. In addition a working trot is allowed for the horse not yet established in collection.

The **canter** is a three-beat movement. It may be performed on either the left or the right 'lead', depending upon the sequence of legs. For example on the right lead, the left hind leg pushes off from the ground, then the right hind and left fore come forwards as a diagonal pair, and finally the right foreleg follows through; this is followed by a moment of suspension. The canter should be light and regular with a very clear three-time beat, a clear flexing of the horse's back and joints and a

good balance. As with the trot, the canter can be also ridden at working, at medium, in collection, and also in extension.

In the **halt** the horse should stand alert, and without fidgeting. He should be balanced with his weight spread evenly over all four legs. He should be ready to move off actively but calmly at the slightest indication from the rider/trainer. These principles should always be kept in mind whether working on the lunge or from the saddle.

Having taught the horse as much as possible in the stable as regards respect for his owner and being obedient, these same principles now need to be installed in the training environment. The horse must go forwards: not fast, not slow, but at the speed that the rider dictates, and also as if it were of his own free will. Then the trainer can work on establishing and enhancing the horse's natural rhythm, whilst also encouraging the horse to develop a carriage, or outline. Lungeing and long reining will prepare the unbacked horse for ridden work, helping him to understand what will be required of him when he is ridden; they are also a very useful means of improving the way of going of a horse that has already been introduced to the rider.

LUNGEING

A young horse is usually lunged before he is long reined and for this initial stage of training a variety of tack is required. Many different types of tack are used for lungeing by different people, but here I will explain only my personal preferences. The horse will need a plain snaffle bridle, with the reins twisted around each other and looped out of the way by tucking them into the throatlash. I tend to connect the lunge line straight to the nearside ring of the bit, because I prefer to feel the horse's mouth

Lungeing tack correctly fitted and ready for work

whilst lungeing in the same way that I would expect to when riding him eventually. The lunge line should be long enough so that it reaches to the outside of a 20-metre circle, and the lunge whip should be long enough to reach and touch the horse with the end of the lash. It is important to keep the whip out of the horse's face, so when not actually lungeing, keep the whip tucked under your arm so it stays out of the way, and take care not to drop it on the floor.

A lunge roller should be used which is padded so it can sit easily on the horse's back without causing him any discomfort, or which can equally as easily sit over the saddle if it is intended to ride the horse after the lungeing session. Obviously in this case it is important to make sure the horse is wearing the correct tack to be ridden in. The roller should be designed in such a way that it is long enough to reach over the saddle, with two girth fixings, one on each side. It should have several ring attachments on it: one that would allow the rein to lie parallel to the ground when connected to the horse's head; one that is a little higher, and another higher still. A pair of large rings are often located at the top of the roller, equivalent to terret rings in driving, but their purpose for dressage is really for passing the reins through in the slightly more advanced long-reining techniques.

Side-reins can be attached from the roller to the horse's bit. Ideally they should be made of solid leather and the clips at the ends should be of a stout design, able to take quite a lot of weight if the horse decides to get a hold and pull. The horse should wear brushing boots on each leg, and the boots should be adequate to cover enough of the fetlock to prevent any accidental brushing, or knocking whilst he is being lunged.

One of the most important things to remember about horses is that potentially they can be extremely dangerous to the person dealing with them; it is therefore always advisable to begin lungeing in an area that is firstly enclosed, and secondly, free from obstructions. And unless you know the horse very well, do not lunge him with other horses around, for obvious safety reasons.

When you start to lunge your horse, it is wise to lead him around the circle he will later be lunged on, to see if he is likely to respond to your basic forward-going aids. Attach the lunge line to the inside of the horse's bit, and organise it in your

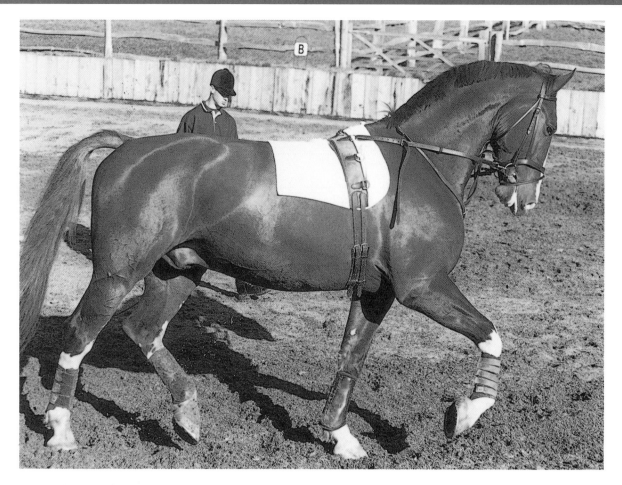

(Above) Going actively forwards, although a little short in the neck in this picture

(Right) A young horse on the lunge; the trainer has a good contact and is obviously walking with the horse. The lunge whip is positioned for minimum disturbance

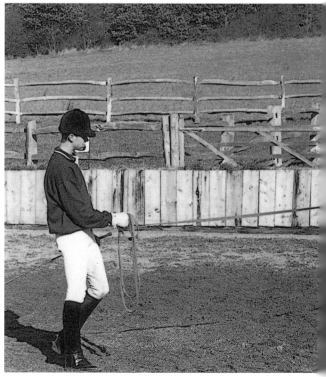

hand in loops of a metre (3ft) or so, making sure that it is not knotted or twisted so that when you begin lungeing it can be released freely and easily. Do not initially set the side-reins up too tightly lest they in any way inhibit the forward movement of the horse, or restrict him; nor should they be so loose that if you draw inwards on the lunge rein, the bit can be pulled through the horse's mouth and cause him discomfort. It is important that both reins are of the same length.

To start the horse off when lungeing, gently push him away from you so that he starts to walk out on the circle, maintaining a feel on the rein the whole time: this contact should be similar to the one you will take up with the reins when eventually you begin riding the horse. Position yourself on the circle roughly level with the horse's girth, and gradually let the lunge line out so that the circle can become bigger. At this stage, in the walk, the circle should be bigger than the length the lunge line will allow, because you should be walking a smaller circle of your own. It is wise to have the horse at a distance from you that is practical for safety reasons and from which the horse will respect what you are doing.

Allow the horse to move freely forwards; do not try to make him wait for you at this stage, as this may inhibit his natural forward thinking. Once he has relaxed and is walking on the circle quite feely, you can move him into trot. Start to flex him a little with the aid of the lunge line and side-reins: by drawing the lunge line into your body, the outside side-rein will come into use, taking more of a contact with the horse's mouth; this should result in the downward or direct flexion of the horse, which is the flexion over his spine. Lateral flexion is the sideways bend along the horse's spine, and it is using the lunge line to draw the horse's head inwards that produces lateral flexion. As the horse places his head and neck more to the inside of the circle, the outside rein will come more into play; and in turn will result in producing more decisive downward flexion.

(Top) Once again the whip is placed behind the trainer so as not to upset the horse

(Above) This horse is unsettled at the beginning of work, which is typical of many youngsters. It is important to allow him to move forwards freely on the circle

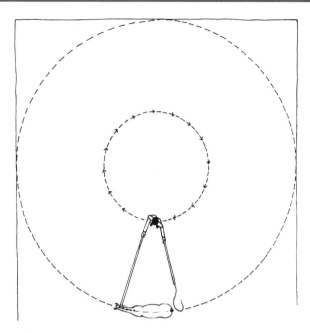

It is not necessary when lungeing to keep the circle static or in the same place, in fact it is preferable that it be moved up and down the school. Thus it is important for the handler not to stand still, but to walk a circle that is large enough to keep the contact with the horse, so that if the horse moves out on the circle, he moves with him, before checking him back. If the horse falls in, adjust the length of the lunge line accordingly to maintain the contact, in order to be able to re-awaken the desire of the horse to go forwards, and to control his rhythm and shape.

To ask the horse to make downward transitions on the lunge, such as trot to walk to halt, do *not* on any account pull him back, or jerk the lunge line. Simply shorten the line, and simultaneously walk towards the horse, using your voice to make him walk. Lead him on *before* he stops and turns in; this will teach him *not* to come suddenly to halt, and spin in and face you. As you ask for the halt transition, walk even closer towards the horse, keeping roughly level with the position of his girth to avoid getting kicked; at no time position yourself in front of his shoulders, or even level with them, so the horse is used to being, and more inclined to be, in front of his handler, rather than behind him.

(Above) This shows the position of the trainer when walking on a larger concentric circle than the horse. This enables him to keep pace with the horse while encouraging him to go forwards
(Below) Although this horse is not yet working through, this picture clearly shows the trainer guiding the horse with a steady contact, whilst his whip is positioned to encourage the horse to move forwards

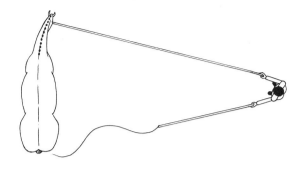

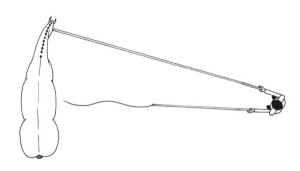

The whip is held behind the horse to encourage him to move actively forwards; (below) the whip position at the middle of the horse will tend to push him out on the circle and will encourage him to increase his bend

I find that it always helps to keep in mind the idea of creating a triangle when lungeing a horse: that is, the triangle that should be formed by the positioning of the lunge line and whip in relation to the horse. The horse should make the base of the triangle, whilst the lunge line and whip form the two sides and the handler makes the apex. If this is kept firmly in mind, you should have maximum control over the horse, because he should be in such a position that it is easy for you to manipulate him, either with the lunge line if he is moving on too fast, or the whip if he is being a little lazy. The horse may initially be rather shy of the whip, in which case keep it tucked behind you until he has settled and only use it when necessary. If the horse tends to fall in on the circle, pointing the whip at his body to create a narrower triangle should prevent him from doing so.

Once the horse is fully loosened up and settled on the lunge, the side-reins can be taken up a little more to improve his level of carriage. The handler can then control his obedience and desire to go forwards, whilst also taking account of his rhythm and adjusting his outline. If the horse starts to pull, just call him to attention as you would if you were riding him. He may become a little deep in front, but this can only really be corrected through increased engagement of his hocks. You may be able to solve this problem temporarily, but in the long run you can't be constantly pulling at the horse and adjusting his way of going; it must become natural for him to move in such a way that his hind legs are engaged, and his front end light. Of course, when you come to ride the horse you will have to make minor corrections, but this is where lungeing can be so useful, in that it prepares the horse so well for ridden work.

The position of your hand controlling the lunge line is terribly important. If you move it forwards, obviously the horse will follow it and move on more. On the other hand, if you move it back into

This horse needs to take his head and neck more forwards, at the same time bringing his hind legs deeper under his body

your body, you will restrict the horse, and he may well slow down. Your bodyweight can also be used to control the horse as you lunge him. If he is pulling at you, counter his pull and make him aware of you by slightly shifting your bodyweight back. Try also to keep your body at a slight angle to the horse, so that your inside shoulder is pointing almost at his inside hip.

When changing the rein, bring the horse back to a walk and get him to halt in the way already discussed. Tuck the whip under your free arm so it is out of the way and unlikely to frighten him whilst you are dealing with him. Unclip the lunge line and quietly swap it over to the other side of the bit; keep hold of the horse by the side-reins in case he decides to move off. The lunge line will need to be swapped over into your other hand: let the slack of it fall to the floor, away from the horse's legs, and as quickly as possible feed it into your other hand. Swap the lunge whip into your other hand by passing it gently behind your back, so as not to alarm the horse. There is no need to alter the side-reins as they should be of equal length, however loose or tight you have them.

When all is ready, push the horse out with either your hand, or whip, encouraging him to walk forwards and out onto the circle. Allow with the hand holding the lunge line, positioning it in front and to the side of your body, which will also encourage the horse to go forwards. When asking the horse to move off be careful not to get too near to him in case he resists; he may even kick inwards with his hind leg in objection to being asked to move off.

To start with, the young horse should be lunged for only short periods of time. When you feel you have actually achieved something, and the horse has obviously improved or learned a lesson, then it is time to stop. Unclip the side-reins conventionally out of the way onto the roller and let the horse walk on freely, so that he can relax his muscles and unwind. It is important to remember that you don't just want to make the horse do what you want, but more beneficially, you want to teach the horse to do willingly what you ask of him. It may take several days, or even several weeks to get the horse settled and into the level of carriage that you require, but this is not a problem. Time spent teaching the horse to become immediately responsive to your aids, and obedient, is certainly not time wasted.

If the horse really starts taking liberties then it is fine to reprimand him, but you don't want to get into

the routine of *punishment* then reward, but rather *reprimand* then reward. The meaning of 'punishment' and of 'reprimand' may hold no significant difference to some people, but to me there is a slightly different intonation. It must be remembered that in the end, you actually want the horse to be on your side, and to work willingly for you. With a very young horse, you will have to take the role of boss at first, but it is important to keep showing him a little kindness so that eventually he learns that complying with what you want of him is far easier and more comfortable. The horse will, however, only get to this stage when he learns to trust you, and is more confident and experienced.

Lungeing the more advanced horse requires, to a certain extent, even greater concentration on the part of the handler. The same basic rules apply, but obviously you are looking for a more advanced state of carriage, and greater engagement of the hindquarters. Again, the horse will be under the control of your voice, and your body positioning.

The contact with the horse's mouth should ideally be 'elastic' and yet definite, and constant. Obviously with the more advanced horse the circle size can be made smaller, since he will still be able to keep his balance and maintain the same degree of collection. In fact the smaller circle can actually help to collect the horse even further.

Even at this level of lungeing, the horse will sometimes get confused as to what you are asking of him. The amount of aid you give the horse is entirely personal, and since the aids themselves are almost identical, relying on the intonation of the voice alone to differentiate between them, a small amount of confusion on the horse's part is bound to arise every now and again.

Having lunged the more advanced horse on perhaps a 12-metre circle, to aid in his collection and engagement he can then be brought onto an even smaller 6-metre circle, or volte, for a short period of time. This will also develop a much more personal relationship between you and the horse, because

In preparation for beginning to long rein rather than lunge, I have made the horse halt and have moved into position behind him. With some horses this momentary 'pause' may be preferable to making an immediate transition from lungeing to long reining

obviously you are much closer to him, and the aids required to make him collect more will be more slight, and perhaps also more frequent. Don't on any account pressure the horse beyond what he is capable of coping with. If he starts to get tense, take him back onto a bigger circle to relax him and establish his rhythm again, before continuing with the work on a smaller circle.

LONG REINING

When the horse is trained to the stage where he accepts and finds it fairly easy to work on a small circle on the lunge, then you can proceed to the next step and this is long reining. It is always a

(Above) I have moved from the centre of the circle to just behind the horse. By adjusting my position I am in the process of changing what was effectively a lunge circle into a circle that I am 'driving' the horse around

(Below) Here the outside rein has just been introduced around the horse's quarters, and is not allowed to become taut; at the same time a steady contact is maintained with the inside rein

good idea to loosen up the horse on the lunge before long reining him, as this will get him listening to your aids before you move on to the more difficult and demanding techniques involved in long reining.

The actual procedure of long reining is fairly simple. It involves the use of two lunge reins, one of which should initially be passed over the horse's neck and clipped to the bit ring on the outside, and the other attached to the inside bit-ring, as it was for lungeing. The type of reins I like to use for this purpose are actually joined together at the buckle. This is useful for when the lunge eventually has to go round the horse's back, which often results in a discrepancy in the length of the two reins, making it easy to drop either one of them. Should this occur, if the two reins are attached by a buckle you won't lose one of them, and if in another situation the outside rein for example needs to be fed out quite a lot, you can just slip past the buckle, giving the horse as much rein as he needs.

Initially, start off lungeing the horse as before, but with the outside rein passed over the horse's neck to the inside; hold both the reins in your leading hand, and the whip as before. The rein can be introduced round the horse's hind legs as soon

as he has comfortably accepted it over the neck. Some horses may panic at this stage, but tactful handling will get the majority of horses over the problem in a couple of moments. Eventually when long reining one might want to use a slightly shorter driving whip than the conventional lungeing whip, but for the moment, when lungeing the horse in preparation for long reining, you still want to be able to reach the horse with the whip. As with lungeing, the side-reins should be fairly loose at this stage, to allow the horse some freedom in his head carriage. With both the left and the right rein, the contact with the horse's mouth should be the same, but later in his training, the outside rein should ideally have a slightly firmer feel, as would be required when riding the horse.

The reins can be used to manipulate the size of the circle that the horse makes. By feeling the outside rein and giving the inside rein, he will move out on the circle, whilst by feeling the inside rein, and giving the outside rein, he will move in. At this stage, the reins should not be passed through the terret rings on the roller, but passed directly to the handler. The side-reins should not be too tight, but at such a length as to allow a little freedom of movement in the horse's head, which will now be controlled to a greater extent by the long reins.

When the horse has become accustomed to the two reins he can then be taken off the circle, and long reined around the school. It is now that the two reins should be passed through the terret rings, and the longer lungeing whip discarded for the shorter driving whip. From the circle, the horse can simply be taken large, staying on the same rein. If he is a little apprehensive about this, increase the size of the circle and gradually introduce him to going straight for a few metres, then bring him back on the circle; this should give him confidence until he is happy to go large.

When going along in a straight line, position yourself slightly on the diagonal behind the horse, and as quietly as possible bring the rein that was resting over the horse's neck up and over, so that it lies parallel with the other rein, passing in a straight

(Left) The newly introduced outside rein is made a little tighter so that the horse can feel its effect. So as not to confuse the horse, the inside rein is slackened slightly for a few moments before being re-introduced

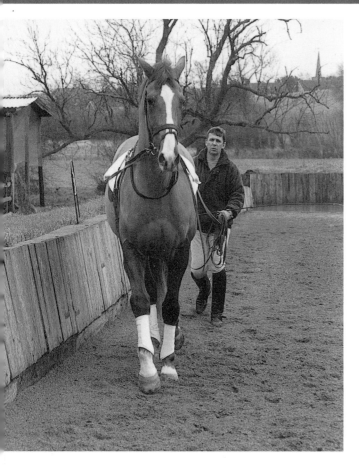

(Above) Here, viewed from both in front and behind, it can be seen clearly that I am positioned behind but, more importantly, slightly to one side of the horse. This is so that a) he can see me; b) should he charge off I am in a position to get him back on the circle rather than be pulled along by him; c) I have a fairly good chance of avoiding any kicks

(Right) Here Bright Spark is feeling fresh and getting a little above himself. It is important in this sort of situation that I don't pull back, but encourage him to move forwards with the voice and driving whip, until he settles

line to your hand. At this stage, be careful not to position yourself directly behind the horse, as he may start to panic if he can't see you, and if he decided to take off, you would be in the worst possible position to control him, as he would have the leverage advantage and the strength to take you. By being slightly on the diagonal, the forward movement of the horse can be controlled if he does take off by bringing him easily back onto the circle. I myself prefer to take large walk steps in preference to running behind the horse, as running may unsettle the horse whilst it also unbalances me, and wears me out quickly.

Try not to let the horse come face to face or even to the wall of the arena when long reining, as he may well become confused and panic. If he steps backwards, simply move back yourself, and use your voice to calm the horse, before progressing forwards once again.

Once the horse has become fully used to being long reined and is at ease with all that is asked of him during long reining, the position of his head and neck can be altered with the use of side-reins and to a lesser extent the long reins. Eventually it should be possible to manipulate the horse's carriage entirely with the use of the long reins, the side-reins having been removed. However, to reach this stage in long reining takes a long time, and can only be developed progressively when both the handler and the horse have a moderate amount of experience.

Changing the rein when long reining is slightly more difficult than doing so when lungeing (see photographic sequences on pp42–3). If, for example, the horse is on the left rein, allow a lot of left rein and shorten the right rein accordingly, so that the horse is directed clearly onto the right rein in a large circle. With practice, the handler will learn to adjust the reins to the right degree. It is at this stage that the horse first feels the rein around his back leg and may become a little tense, or worried. In this case, allow the rein to trail slightly, so that it does not interfere with the horse too much. Don't be afraid of hurting the horse if the rein does get caught between the legs, and equally don't be alarmed if the outside rein rides up under the horse's tail. The material of the reins should be such that it is heavy enough to drop back down to its ordinary position under its own weight.

It is important to keep the inside bend slightly, as this will allow the handler more control over the horse, and may help to prevent him rushing away or taking too strong a hold of the bit. If the reins get slightly muddled or twisted, adjust them quietly, at a convenient time; if the horse is misbehaving, just leave them until he has settled, as fiddling with them at a time like this may mean losing control of him.

Things don't always go according to plan!

Initially when long reining the horse in straight lines, use the positioning of your body to keep him straight. If for example the horse falls to the outside, move yourself further to the outside to counter his movement, and he should move back to travelling in a straight line. The positioning of your body in relation to the horse can also help when introducing lateral work whilst long reining.

These sequences show how I position myself in relation to the horse when changing the rein in long reining, from in front and behind

The shoulder-in can be developed by taking the horse large from a circle, and positioning yourself slightly to the outside of the horse. If the horse starts to fall in, take him back onto the circle, and attempt the movement again. Similarly, leg-yielding and half-pass can be taught to the horse, initially in walk, and then in trot. The rein-back can also be introduced when long reining: ask for only very few steps at a time to start with, because you don't want the horse rushing back, and resume the forward movement before the horse gets too close to you.

In the case of very advanced horses, long-reining techniques can be used to enhance some of the work you do when riding the horse. For

example, the piaffe and passage can be greatly improved with work on the long reins, whilst also giving the rider a good opportunity to study the horse's movements from the ground. It is necessary to get slightly closer to the horse when practising these movements, to get a clearer feeling of the contact with his mouth, and you must therefore be even more aware of the possibility that he might kick out with his back legs at this stage.

In summary, lungeing and long-reining techniques are very valuable practices in the training of a young horse, preparing him well for when he is ridden. These techniques can also help older horses that have commenced their ridden training, consolidating and improving the work that has already been taught to them; and they can help the rider in his day-to-day riding and in his appreciation of his horse.

Whilst this horse is slightly on the forehand, he is clearly getting into the swing of things

What if the horse turns in and tries to face me on the lunge?

This is a problem which usually occurs when the horse is first lunged. To prevent it happening, it is very important to position yourself correctly in relation to the horse right from the start of the lungeing process. If the horse still tries to turn in and won't take an even contact on the lunge line, refusing to keep a constant tension between his mouth and your hand, curl up the lunge line carefully in your hand and hold it close to the bit, and so lead the horse along. Thus, if you are on the left rein and holding the lunge line in your left hand, in effect your left arm is crossed over your body. Hold the whip in reverse in your right hand, so that you can simply reach behind and gently touch the horse's side with the handle end. Whilst doing this, you should be walking forwards on a large circle, of a similar size to the one you would wish the horse to be on when he is eventually lunged in the usual way.

As you walk forwards, push the horse away from you with the whip, using it either on his shoulder or girth area and as firmly as is necessary to make him react to you without upsetting him. At the same time as you push him away from you with the whip, allow the lunge line to come steadily out of your hand. This must, however, be done in such a way that the *horse* is the one stepping out and taking up the contact, until he is walking a larger circle than you. The size of the circle that you are walking on can then be reduced, leaving you in a good position to start pushing the horse forwards on the lunge in the normal way, once he has accepted the contact.

If the horse repeatedly turns in and drops the contact, then this exercise of leading him with the whip behind you should be practised until he learns not to. You

Here the horse is attempting to turn in to face me, so I have slackened the lunge line and have taken the whip more behind him to re-establish his desire to move forwards around the circle again

will eventually teach him not to do this; but it is no use giving up after a couple of attempts, because then he will think he can get away with it.

What if the horse misbehaves and ignores the use of the lunge whip?

This problem usually arises when the horse is aware that you cannot influence or reach him with the lash of the lunge whip when you use it; it is a situation that concerns his respect for the aids, rather than the trainer's over-use of them. The lunge whip should be used between the horse's elbow and haunches, and never in a sharp way unless it is necessary to reprimand him for being disobedient or not paying attention. However, in general the whip should be used in a light, flicking way so that the end of the lash just touches lightly against the horse's side. Some horses will be a little slow in reacting to this, whilst others will over-react. It is therefore up to you to establish how often and how severely you should use the whip, according to the nature of the horse you are lungeing.

What if my horse turns away from me and rushes off out of the circle on the lunge?

This is a slightly more worrying, not to mention dangerous, problem than when the horse merely turns in on the circle. If he manages to turn his head away from you completely, there is actually very little you can do to stop him running away. It is therefore most important to prevent him getting to this stage: prevention is a lot better than cure, particularly in this instance.

Make sure you are always out of reach of his hooves. It is very easy

for the horse to turn out, swing his quarters in towards you, and cow kick; a potentially dangerous situation that must also be considered as a possible reality. Position yourself correctly, and keep a careful eye on his demeanour so you can anticipate any signs of trouble.

Keep the horse on a small circle approximately 2–3 metres away from you, whilst you walk on a 10-metre circle. This should not be too much of a problem, because the sort of horse prone to this type of behaviour will undoubtedly be one which travels forwards easily – it is when you allow him to get too far away from you that he can turn away easily. By keeping him on his 12–13 metre circle with his head held quietly to the inside, you will have much more control over his actions. As you become more confident, gradually increase the size of the circle; then bring him back in to you again, making the circle smaller. In this way he will get used to being taken onto a small circle, let out onto a larger one, and then taken back in again. In this instance, try to anticipate when the horse is liable to turn around and rush off, use your common sense, and decrease the size of the circle.

Some books advocate putting poles on the ground to correct a horse that rushes out on the lunge; I don't like this practice myself, since I believe it could lead to a very dangerous situation, with the horse perhaps getting a jump pole stuck between his legs. However, if you do have an enclosed schooling area, by all means move yourself into one of the corners so that at least two sides of your circle are enclosed by the sides of the school;

you will therefore only have to cope with the other two corners on which the horse could turn out. When the horse behaves and listens to you in one corner, you could quietly move him along into another corner just by repeating the aids required to keep him on the circle again and again. Here, as with the problem of the horse turning in, the solution really lies once again in being persistent.

What if my horse refuses to go forwards on the lunge line?

This problem may occur if the horse gets himself into a panic situation, such as has just been described, or he may have learned to nap, in that he stands still, plants his feet and simply refuses to move on. It is one which seems to arise by no means infrequently. It may help to approach within sensible reach of the horse to encourage him forwards. Horses that get very uptight stand with their backs hollowed and their legs spread underneath them. When the horse is in such a state, you have to be careful that you don't make the problem worse. Nevertheless, you have to try to encourage him to go forwards. If you have checked that the side-reins are not too tight, and if there is no obvious reason why the horse should not move forwards, then you must encourage him to take forward steps.

This doesn't mean immediately setting about him with the lunge whip. Instead, place yourself in a position whereby you can drop the lash not too harshly on his flank, quarters, or just below his hocks. Every horse will react differently to the touch of the whip on the different parts of his body, and by flicking the whip in these different places you can find where he is most sensitive. Then, flick him repeatedly until he reacts, whether this means that he simply moves forwards, or bucks and gallops off. Whichever it is, reward him with a kind word. This may seem somewhat inappropriate if he canters off pulling like a tank, but nonetheless, it is still important that he isn't just made to go forwards, but is persuaded to *want* to go forwards.

Having said this, I have actually been obliged to stand for ages with horses that are really obstinate and have dug their hooves firmly into the ground, and at times like this the horse has to feel more than a little tap around his backside to persuade him to move forwards. However, even if it is necessary to use the whip a little harder, the severity with which you use it must still be carefully judged, with the best interests of the horse always being kept in mind. If you do end up having to give him a crack around the back end in order to send him on, make sure that you have left the way open so that he can go on, by releasing your hand and guiding him forwards; and then equally importantly, make sure that you make a big fuss of him verbally once he has established his forward movement, so that he understands that this was a reprimand, and not just a senseless punishment. Punishments should never be administered purely for you to get your own back on the horse, but always with a view to teaching the horse what you require of him, and thereby improving him.

How do I know how long or short to have the side-reins?
The side-reins should never be fixed too tightly. With a more advanced horse it may be possible to start off with the side-reins a lot shorter, especially if it is a horse you know. With an unfamiliar animal, or one which is very young, it is wise to start off with longer side-reins. All the time, the reins should be taken up just enough for you to have a contact with the horse's mouth. If the horse is particularly stiff to one side, I rarely advocate shortening the inside side-rein when the horse is travelling in this direction as a way to achieve more bend; ideally he should be pushed up into his body so that he gives the correct bend naturally.

If you leave the side-reins too long, they will have no effect on the horse's way of going. The lunge line will take up all the contact against one side of the horse's mouth, depending which rein he is on, and the bit may therefore be pulled through the mouth. If, however, you make sure that the outside rein is short enough so that when there is a contact on the lunge line, the outside rein comes into play, the pressure of this outside rein can then be matched by adjusting the

The side-reins: (from top to bottom) too short; too long; correctly fitted

inside rein; when this is achieved, you will know that you have the side-reins at roughly the correct length for the horse's way of going. Obviously as the work progresses, you will ask for more engagement of the back end and it is then permissible to shorten the side-reins further.

It must be remembered that side-reins do not necessarily help with horses that tend to rush in and out on the circle. Their use is not to hold the horse on the circle, but rather to encourage him, together with the correct way of sending him forwards, so that he comes up and actually takes the contact, whilst moving forwards. In most cases it is a mistake to tie down the horse's head to stop him rushing either one way or another on the circle, because eventually he will learn to step behind the bit and escape anyway. For example, he may react violently by coming to a halt and rearing up against the action of the side-reins.

What if my horse resists the contact imposed on him by the side-reins?

A problem such as this may manifest itself in the horse refusing to go forwards, or he may go backwards, or worse still, he may try to stand up in resistance to the side-reins. An obvious reason for this is that the side-reins provide too tight a contact with the horse's mouth, and probably too early in his introduction to lungeing. Alternatively, he may just suddenly become panicky or claustrophobic, and because he is an uptight sort of horse, all at once he takes exception to the action of the side-reins. As you become more

experienced at lungeing, however, you will see these problems building up before they develop to the stage that is now being discussed.

When starting to introduce young or sensitive horses to side-reins, attach the end of the reins to a ring high up on the roller, near the wither. The main reason for this is that if the horse does become panicked by feeling the reins too tight, he will tend to hollow his neck and come above the rein. If, by having the reins attached in such a way, it is possible for the horse to do this, he can release the tension on the reins by putting his head up higher, and this may prevent him rearing and going over backwards. If, on the other hand, the side-reins are down low, the higher the horse raises his head, the tighter the reins will become and thus he may well end up rushing backwards to try to release himself from the pressure of them. Alternatively, he may fall over onto his side; something which should on all accounts be avoided if you don't want to damage his confidence.

Again, the answer here really lies in prevention rather than cure, namely by not doing up the reins too tightly, too soon. However, once the problem has actually occurred, all you can do is loosen the lunge line, lead the horse forwards with the hand that is holding the lunge rein, and encourage him forwards with the lunge whip. Do this carefully, as too violent an action with the lunge whip will actually exacerbate the problem and cause the horse to run backwards at an even faster rate. Another solution is simply to move quietly towards the horse and undo the side-reins; although this will be almost

impossible to accomplish if the horse has locked himself against the reins, because the clip will be extremely hard to unfasten. Even if you can pull the draw-clip back, it will be very difficult to undo and to release the horse without throwing him into a further panic. It is for this reason that I therefore never buckle up the side-reins too tightly, and I always have them loose enough to be able to release them should an awkward situation arise. It is for this reason also that I don't tuck the loose ends of the side-reins in the keepers, and if I do, I certainly don't make them secure so that if necessary they can be undone easily. If you are into this stage of the problem, it is usually sufficient to release just one of the side-reins until the horse relaxes, then release the other.

If you do employ this method of easing the pressure on the horse, it is important not to get too close to him without being very aware of the fact that he may still panic. A kind word may reassure him, but even so, look after yourself in this situation so that you don't end up with the horse coming down on top of you. Again, I will reiterate that these problems shouldn't arise if everything is done correctly. However, in the real world we all make mistakes sometimes, and it is therefore useful to have a solution to these problems; I hope the ones I have suggested may help you out of any awkward situation. With driving horses, and particularly in teams, many people actually carry a sharp knife to deal with this kind of problem, so that if a horse gets really tangled up, or panics, then it can be cut loose. This does not necessarily mean that we should carry a knife each time we lunge a horse, but it is interesting to know that trainers in the driving world do so, for obvious safety reasons.

What if my lines get tangled up when I am long reining?

This is a problem anyone could encounter when long reining, especially someone not very experienced. It can be quite confusing having to control two lines, and the lunge whip, as well as the horse, and maintain some resemblance of order, but really the only way to practise controlling all these factors is to get out there and do it yourself. Take the chance that you will make mistakes and that the horse will get muddled up – problems such as this do happen from time to time, and obviously you will do the best you can to avoid them; and with experience they will occur less and less.

The main thing to remember is initially to trust only the line that would be your lunge line. So, for example, if you were lungeing to the left, the line that goes directly to the horse's mouth with your left hand is the line that is the most important, and the outside rein is very much the auxiliary rein. If the worst came to the worst and you lost contact with the outside rein completely, you would still have the greater amount of control with the left rein, or vice versa if the horse is on the other rein. Start off by passing the outside rein back over the horse's neck, because the discrepancy of the reins will then be much less than if it was around his back end. Like this, the chance of everything getting tangled up will be that much less.

In fact, as I have already explained, I use my lunge lines joined together, making the process of moving from one rein to another a lot easier. When a horse is being introduced to the long reins, he may run away from the one that is put around his back end for the first time; all you can do in this situation is let this rein out, even to the point where it may drag slightly on the floor. In this way there will be minimum pressure around the horse's quarters, and he will be less likely to run away.

If the horse should spin round and face you so that all the reins get into a mess, don't panic. Just gently draw the horse in towards you, and if you have to, unclip just one of the reins, keeping the other clipped on. Let it fall to the floor, but make sure you walk the horse away from the rein. Then simply start again. Pick up the rein, coiling it up so that it is suitable for use, and clip it back on to the horse again. It is quite common for people to give up long reining very early on because they have got tangled up once or twice and have therefore become a little nervous about the situation. And naturally it is fairly offputting when there is a heavyweight horse leaping around, not to mention the lunge lines flying everywhere; but the only way to become an expert is with experience, by practising.

When learning the procedures of long reining make sure you have someone at hand who knows how to deal with the problems, and who will help you should you get into trouble. In fact long reining really isn't as hard as it is often made out to be – perhaps some of the concepts are quite difficult to comprehend but just remain logical; think about where the problems lie, and what you can do about them if they occur.

What if the outside line gets tangled up and comes between the horse's legs?

As long as the horse is not too bothered by this it is not a great problem, and you can actually use a bit of both the inside and outside reins to bring him quietly to a halt. Get your assistant to stand at his head thus leaving you free to untangle the line, taking care that the horse doesn't kick you in the process. However, if he is getting really fraught, it is most probably because the long rein is being held too firmly against his legs due to the fact that you have failed to release the pressure on it once it has become positioned here. A simple solution is to maintain the contact on the direct rein and to let the other rein just go slack; if it falls to the ground the horse should just travel either past it or over it. It may trail behind the horse, but this shouldn't cause any great problem. Bring the horse back to halt and collect the rein up, then commence where you left off.

It may seem that in many of these situations I keep telling you to stop, and only to start again once the problem has been solved. However, it is the best way to collect your thoughts, and to think ahead and plan what you are going to do, rather than reacting to everything in such a way that you lose your co-ordination and lose sight of what you are trying to achieve. The aim of long reining is for it to be an enjoyable, fun experience for the horse, and by quietly working and solving the problems, the answers will be found that much more quickly than if you 'chase' him, trying to do too much, too soon.

3

RIDING CIRCLES, STRAIGHT LINES AND TRANSITIONS

CIRCLES

Backing and lungeing the horse will have entailed working him on a circle, so it is logical that when you first start working him off the lunge, you begin the work on a circle. All too often people get on young horses and ride them in straight lines. However, I believe that initially a horse should be worked in the way that he is accustomed to, and that by working on a circle his balance and self-carriage can be better established, making later work on straight lines relatively easy.

The important thing to remember about working on circles is that you make it as easy and as comfortable as possible for the horse. If you have been lungeing him on a 15–20 metre circle, then on no account must you make the ridden circles any smaller than this. The horse will find it difficult enough learning to cope with his own balance, and to put a rider on his back will upset his natural balance even more. It is therefore a good idea to start the ridden work when the horse is still on the lunge, so the size of the circle can be controlled by the trainer, whilst the rider just sits quietly on the horse's back, not having to influence him in any way. Once the horse has learned to cope with the weight of the rider, the lunge line can be released, and the horse ridden independently on the circle, in walk, trot, and eventually canter.

Because the basics have been soundly established on the lunge and by long reining, the horse should by this stage understand the aids for stopping, starting, and turning left and right. He should have no fear of a contact with his mouth, or of being sent on by the voice. Although a particularly sharp horse may be initially concerned

A green young horse on a corner: four-year-old Itis

about the rider's legs, the ridden work can nevertheless be commenced with the horse fully prepared to accept your basic aids. The fact that you can apply these aids in walk, trot or canter is secondary to the fact that the horse trusts you enough to allow you to increase the speed and then to slow down.

This trust is the golden thread which runs through a horse's training, so that you and he come to an understanding that you are not going to harm him, and thus he will allow you to manipulate him to a certain extent. Because he comes to trust you enough to know that he will not experience any discomfort, he will then be more inclined to co-operate in a situation which he is a little nervous about.

When I start riding a young horse I often use an open rein, that is, I slightly lead him in the direction I want him to go. For example, when on a circle I may have to open the outside rein to lead him to the outside of the circle, rather than just pulling his mouth; in addition, a slight shifting of the bodyweight in this direction will enhance the aid. The rider must be careful not to put any downward pressure on the young horse's back; concentrate the weight on the stirrup iron, rather than sitting deep in the saddle. Using your seat as a training aid can be introduced much later on, when the horse's back has come up in such a way that he has enough strength to carry your weight. If you attempt to sit on a horse's back that is in any way flat or hollowed, whether this be through weakness or nervous tension, you will cause him discomfort in this area, which in turn will cause him to produce a defence or resistance to what you are asking him to do.

Therefore when you begin work on the circle, your weight on the horse should be disposed not so much into the centre of the horse's back but down your legs, and down the horse's sides. This allows the horse to know where you are, and to be able to receive your leg aids clearly, whilst it also enables you to feel the movements of the horse effectively, and to anticipate his next actions.

A lot of people when they begin riding a young horse will do so on an extremely loose rein, a practice that I don't entirely agree with. To my mind, the reins should be of a contact that allows both horse and rider to feel each other. The contact established will obviously vary with each horse: some horses are a little bit heavier in their general acceptance of the aids, but even the lightest horse will be heavy at moments, and too light at others. However, a continual contact must be established through your seat, leg and hand in this order of priority, so that the horse knows exactly where you are and what you are asking him to do. If habitually you have a very slack rein and your legs have no real contact with his sides, by suddenly putting your leg on, you will most probably give him quite a surprise, and this will undermine his confidence in you as a rider and in what you are asking of him, possibly to the extent where he starts building up resistances.

The rider's position is of paramount importance. He must have developed his abilities sufficiently so

The rider must learn to achieve and maintain a good seat and position

that he does not in any way disturb the young horse in its way of going, and he must be balanced enough to be able to influence the horse without provoking resistances, and making him defensive; although whilst still on the lunge, he should remember to remain relatively ineffective, with the horse's way of going and the size of the circle being controlled by the trainer. This will enable the horse to get used to the feel of a rider on his back, and similarly, for the rider to get used to the feel of the horse.

At this stage it is extremely important for both rider and trainer to use a lot of voice so as to engage the horse's attention. When training horses that are slightly sharp and may have a tendency to spook, try not be too quick to tell them off. Instead,

concentrate your efforts on refocusing the horse's attention back on you, as his spooking will have been due to a loss of concentration on the rider. It is unreasonable to expect a very young horse to maintain concentration for very long, as it is also with a young child; a fact which must be taken into consideration in the training. *Little and often* is the key practice to remember. It is much better to gain the horse's attention fully for a short period of time, so that this time is wholly productive and can be ended with the satisfaction that you have really taught him something, rather than making him do what you want through bullying tactics.

In short, your early training of the horse is rather like teaching him a language. For example, when riding a circle, and taking the classical application of the aids, the 'dialogue' would be the inside leg on the girth, the outside leg behind the girth, the inside rein applied to help the bend, and the outside rein to contain the bend and control the horse. The difference between all the aids required in dressage – such as the canter aid, or the aid for a half-pass – is really only in the emphasis placed upon them. None of these aids can be clearly distinguished, or categorised one from another. The horse therefore has to learn to differentiate between very slight variances in the aids applied; be this a variance in pressure, or in the positioning of, for example, the rider's legs.

Horses are actually very perceptive to the aids and any movements made by the rider, and if asked correctly, they will give willingly what is required of them; but if they misunderstand the rider's request, they are just as likely to build up defences. It is therefore the responsibility of the rider and trainer at this stage to minimise any misunderstandings by being very clear and concise in what they ask of the horse.

Start by walking the circle. The primary requirement here is that the horse walks on, and even if the walk is a little on the hurried side, do not try to alter it too much. For me, an enthusiastic, forward-thinking walk that is actually taking you somewhere is one to be valued, and not meddled with. If the horse is hesitant in his walk and not taking fully enthusiastic strides, he will start looking for something else to do, and the focus of

Daniel Timson and Bright Spark doing a 10m circle showing good bend and activity, although the engagement could be greater

his attention will perhaps shift away from his rider.

When the horse is happy to walk freely forwards and to accept the basic turning and stopping aids, so that he can be asked to stand still and walk on again, or move in and out on the circle without offering any resistances, the trot work can be commenced. This may cause problems in the walk, in that the horse may start putting in a few jog strides; but it is a problem for which I do not in any way punish him, least of all at this level. Allow him to jog for a few strides and then ask him to come quietly back to walk. Again, this particular problem originates in the horse's misinterpretation of emphasis. If you have asked him to go forwards and he trots, he has actually responded to what you have asked of him. That you wanted perhaps a more active walk, and not a jog, is a minor problem, which can be corrected later on in his training. At this stage the fact that the horse goes forwards in response to your aids is of primary importance. This particular mistake must be looked upon as a sign of obedience.

Another problem that may occur once you start trot work, is that the horse may break into canter, although this is no serious offence as long as he doesn't become out of control. As with the jogging, allow him to canter for a few strides, and then gently ask him to come back to trot through a series of repeated aids, rather than one prolonged aid. This repetitive aid, which may involve asking perhaps five or six times before getting the reaction that you want, saves you from having to increase the physical strength of your aid. It is only too easy to start increasing the strength of your aids, rather than relying on the soft repeated aid that in the long run will produce a light and receptive horse.

Obviously a good seat and sense of balance will help you immensely in the application of these subtle aids. Even riders who are still learning to develop this seat and balance, if correctly guided by a trainer – who will have most of the control because he has the horse on the lunge – can improve the riding techniques required for a young horse. The balance required by the rider for young horses is a fairly acute one, because you have to be able to react very quickly, but without being abrupt, to changes in the horse's way of going.

Having got the horse into trot, I will always initially ride in sitting trot, albeit very lightly. By this I do not mean sitting into the horse's back, but rather, keeping a little bit of weight off the horse's back, and distributing most of your weight into your legs, and the stirrups irons. The horse mustn't find your weight too much of a shock, and I have found that if you start off in rising trot this can often disturb horses much more than by sitting, and just letting the horse gently feel your weight constantly on his back. The trot at this stage may be rather erratic and uncomfortable, but try to sit as evenly and as quietly as possible.

Once the initial forward movement is established, the rising trot can then be introduced, and can actually become extremely useful. In my opinion it is best to sit as the outside foreleg comes back on the right rein; this would be the left foreleg (the horse's near fore) and you would rise on the right diagonal. There are some trainers and schools that teach their pupils to sit as the inside foreleg comes back, a practice which is open to discussion; but on the whole, sitting as the outside foreleg comes back, and rising as the inside foreleg goes forwards, is the method most practised. Keeping your balance is the primary requirement in the rising trot, so that the horse moves obediently, without offering any resistances, and trots forwards without rushing.

A forward-going trot is one in which the horse enthusiastically takes strides in the direction in which he is being asked, and at the speed at which he is being asked to move on. It is important that the pace which you set for the horse to trot at is self-sustaining, and not artificially fast or slow. The analogy I like to use for this is the speed that you would like to have if you were on a bicycle, in that if you are freewheeling, you don't want to be rushing down the hill hanging on to the brakes, and neither do you want to be pushing too hard going up the hill. You must therefore do as much pushing or pedalling as is necessary to cause the horse to move energetically. Such a dynamic situation will be changing all the time: thus, a sluggish horse will be wanting to slow the speed all the time, and the rider must be careful not to push him constantly, but rather to provoke him into reacting to you by using one slightly sharper leg aid, and then continuing with your legs as normal. With the sharper horse that tries to rush forwards all the time, his speed should be checked by repeated actions with your reins, and by positioning your bodyweight down into your stirrup irons.

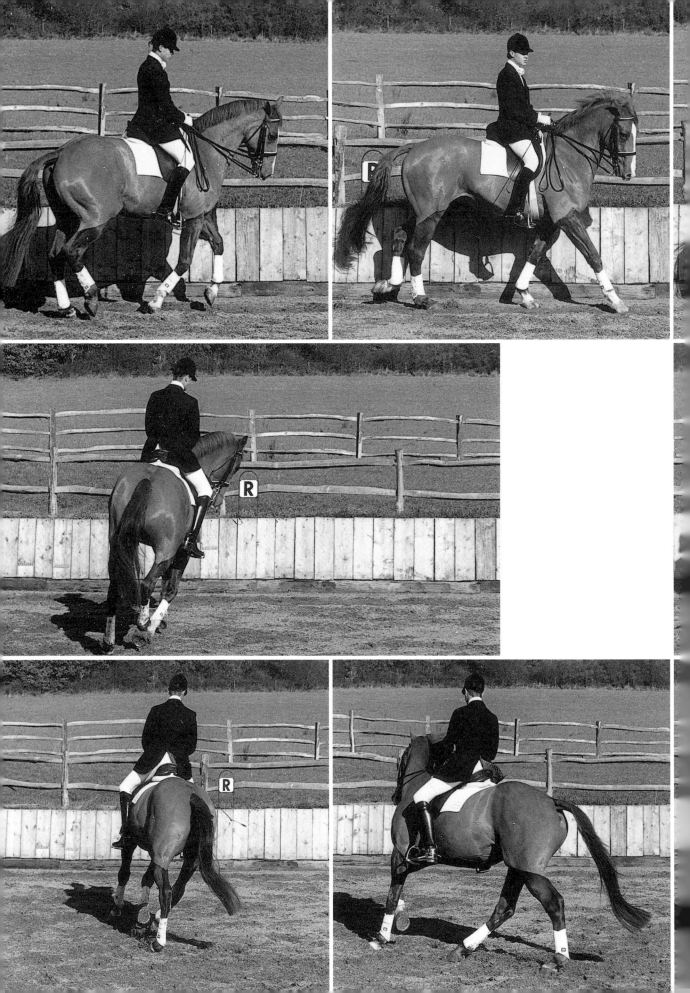

At this level of training, 'forwards' is therefore very much the idea that you are progressing in the direction that you want to go, and in the manner in which you wish to be travelling, but also, quite importantly, with the minimum of effort on your part in maintaining and sustaining the horse's desire to move forwards. If you have to cause the horse to react to you by asking him to go faster or slower, what you must avoid is to keep pulling back, or kicking on. Instead, the horse must be made to listen to you by a slightly sharper action of the leg or rein; not made to go faster or slower. Although only a minor difference in terminology, this idea implies a large difference in the intention of the rider. For example, my first aid to make a horse go forwards would never be a kick, but if he persists in being sluggish I may well kick him quite firmly, possibly followed up by use of the schooling whip, to make him react to me, so that subsequently he will respond to the light aids which I would normally apply.

The next stage of schooling your horse on the circle is to move into canter. As with walk and trot, attempt it first on the lunge, before riding the horse independently. From observing horses in the field I have found that they never actually canter unless either spooked, or if they run out of speed in the trot. If the horse is spooked, he will most likely turn on his heel and leave the area as fast as possible; but if, for example, he is travelling along with a group of horses, he will generally tend to trot until he reaches the maximum speed at which this pace allows him to travel, at which point he will break into canter.

Knowing this, the rider can therefore utilise the natural way of going of the horse to establish the canter initially. Thus, when riding along in rising trot, simply increase the speed of the trot very gradually, until the point where experience will indicate to you that the horse is likely to break into canter in the next couple of strides. At this point the canter aid can be applied to enhance the horse's transition. Take the outside leg back, feel the outside rein, and keep the inside bend. In this way the horse will soon learn to associate your aids with the canter transition, and I find that in only a few days, the canter can be achieved from a trot of the

Daniel and Bright Spark on a 10m canter circle

normal speed, as long as it is bright and active. Similarly, the same method can be used for walk to canter transitions. Slightly hurry the speed of the walk until it is a little faster than the speed you would normally desire, and then apply the canter aid. At first the horse probably will produce a few trot strides before cantering, but in time, and with consistent application of the aid, the horse will progressively learn to accept the aid from the pace that you are in, and to go into the pace at which you wish him to be in.

All the time that I am asking the horse to move forwards, I also move him a little bit sideways in a subtle, inoffensive way, by putting a small amount of inside leg on, treading lightly on the outside stirrup, feeling the outside rein, and letting the size of the circle that I am riding him on become a bit bigger. The circle size can then be decreased by leading the horse in with the inside hand, with a little bodyweight also to the inside. If too much bodyweight is applied in this one direction, you may throw the horse off balance, and in response he will move in the opposite direction. It is therefore a matter of proportions; and how much or how little weight is needed can be learned through practice, by trial and error.

Whilst asking the horse to move forwards and sideways, you must apply your aids in the correct order of priority. Firstly the horse should be obedient, if only in the most basic terms, in that he is safe to ride. Secondly, as I have already said, he should be progressing forwards in an enthusiastic way, but without being over-enthusiastic so that he is rushing or running; and thirdly, he must be moving in a rhythm that allows you to follow his beat. Obviously the horse has his own mechanical rhythm; for example the walk is four-beat, the trot two-beat, and the canter three-beat. However, depending on the nature of the horse and the way he reacts to the rider, this rhythm may not be maintained, and it may also be difficult for the rider to establish this rhythm in his mind.

To make things slightly easier, the walk, for example, can be counted as one beat for every four steps the horse takes, and if the rider firmly embodies this simple rhythm in his mind, it may well help with maintaining the natural rhythm of the horse. This same technique can be applied also to the trot, which has a fairly rapid two-beat rhythm, that may have the tendency to make the

rider chase the horse, rather than listen to him. What therefore needs to be found is a way of following the horse's stride that doesn't rush either rider or horse. This is especially important with a young horse, which will need a moderate amount of time to take in, and respond to, what is being asked of him. Some horses have very large trot strides, making it easier for the rider to decipher the rhythm. The majority of horses, however, have a stride that will become quicker and more hassled if they are pushed on, and will thus lose rhythm, making it difficult for the rider to keep the two-tempo established in his mind. It may therefore be useful to count one beat for every two, or even four, trot strides.

The canter rhythm is slightly more complex, being a three-beat movement; for the rider to count out each beat would at best make riding the canter rather hectic. What I find helps in this respect is to categorise the strides into groups of four, so that for the first three-beat, you count one, and for the next, two, and so on until the fourth three-beat which can be counted as four, and then back to one again. A sensible beat can thus be established, that allows the horse to respond to you, and you to respond to the horse, without being under the pressure of having to maintain a beat which you can barely keep up with. Another advantage of establishing such a rhythm is that it will allow the horse to cover more ground because you will be giving him more distance in which to achieve what you want him to do.

STRAIGHT LINES

Having now trained your horse to work evenly and freely on a circle, he should be ready to start work on straight lines. He should be somewhat prepared for this, in that he should have been circled in every part of the arena and not just around one particular area, and so he will be used to the environment he is working in. In addition he should be mobile, and used to working with a bend and with a certain degree of self-carriage, or balance, making the progression to 'going large' a fairly natural one.

Firstly establish your circle, preferably one of 20 metres in size (the width of the school) so that on reaching the edge of the arena, you can simply carry on up the long side for several metres, confirmed this well enough, he can then be asked to counter-flex; in other words, to bend to the outside whilst still on the circle, so that a lateral flexibility is achieved. Whilst young, and to a certain extent when the horse is more advanced, he should be positioned to the inside, so that a slight curve through the whole of his body is made to the inside.

For me, straightness in a horse does not, as it may imply, mean that he is rigidly straight like a board, but straight in that he carries himself in a straight line, and gives the appearance to someone watching him that he is straight. Thus, even in the case of more advanced horses, I find that it often gives them confidence if the bend that they have established is maintained throughout all their movements. For example, imagine riding down a centre line: as you approach the end of the line, the horse may start to wander and even get quite anxious, if he doesn't know which way you want him to turn; eventually, he may well make up his

Kirsty Mepham and Dikkiloo: an advanced horse showing slight positioning to the inside, whilst remaining perfectly straight

depending on how the horse is responding to being ridden straight. Maintain the degree of the horse's inside bend that was established on the circle, even though this may be a more exaggerated bend than you would eventually want. The rider must be very aware of the horse's actions at this point, so that before he starts to lose his balance, or bend, he must be taken onto the circle. In this way the horse's confidence will be increased, and gradually, he can be taught to work in a straight line for a longer distance, until he is happy to go the whole way around the arena.

Having established the horse's forward movement, in a suitable rhythm, we then move on to the subject of his 'shape'. When on a circle, the first stage in getting him 'shaped' – that is to say, into an outline that will enable him to establish his balance more easily – is asking him to bend laterally to the inside. When the horse has

Optimist in a good straight line with Dane during a Grand Prix test

The advanced horse: Jackie Bickley and The Rooster show a good example of a horse in self-carriage on a straight line

own mind about the direction in which he goes, and is likely to dive round the turn at the top. However, if a horse is used to being positioned in anticipation of the direction he is to turn, he will learn to recognise which way he is being required to go, and won't become tense about the turn in any way.

So as you go down the centre line intending to turn left, have the horse very slightly positioned to the left, aided by a little bit of feel on the outside rein. When you come to the end the horse should therefore be confident that the turn will be made to the left. If on the other hand, you enter the centre line on the left rein, but are intending to turn right, the horse needs his positioning to be changed to the right. This should be done approximately half-way down the centre line, so that he has sufficient warning as to which direction is to be taken at the end. Again, this will help to increase the confidence between horse and rider, and build up the so-called 'dialogue' between them.

Once the horse is, we would hope, happy to go forwards in an established rhythm and in a suitable shape, in that he bends to the inside of whichever direction he is travelling, the rider can now start to demand from him that he flexes over his top line. However, if you have been working the horse forwards in an active, bright manner, without running him out of his balance and with the correct bend, you will invariably find that the horse starts to offer you direct flexion. In other words he will start to carry his head and neck in a rounded way, which allows his back to round, and his strides to become more springy.

The outline of the horse can thus be categorised into two parts: primarily the lateral flexing of the horse to the left or right, and secondly, the downward flexion of the top line. If you have a horse that accepts the flexion, but is absolutely dead straight, it will take very little disturbance for him to hollow. If, on the other hand, he has a little position to the inside, he will accept the flexion of his poll much more readily, particularly when the positioning is applied correctly from the back of his body to the front of it, and he is ridden through from the seat and leg, before using the hand. Training the horse in such a way will lead to his 'throughness', a term used frequently in dressage. It is a feeling that the horse is moving *actively* forwards, pushing and carrying himself off his hocks, and stepping in a basculed, or rounded, shape through his back to the hand, whilst accepting both the lateral flexion – that is, the sideways flexion – and the direct flexion, the flexing of the poll.

In the case of younger horses, you may well work them in a slightly lower outline, but as their ability to carry more weight on the back end increases, they should eventually push through more from behind with their back legs, lighten their shoulders, and come up to a position where the poll becomes more or less the highest point of the neck.

Let us return to the subject of working the horse through corners. We must now consider the size of corners that we are going to ask him to negotiate. For me, teaching the young horse how to negotiate corners in a geometrically correct way is a very important part of his education. If he is only just able to balance himself on a large 20-metre circle, then the corners you ride on him should be only one quarter of a 20-metre circle in size. It is common to feel that the corners should be ridden fairly tightly and this is quite correct in the later stages of training of the horse, but at this early stage, they should be kept shallow, so that the horse can successfully keep his balance. It is only when the horse can quite easily cope with a 15- or even 10-metre circle, and fully keep his balance, that corners of these tight dimensions can be ridden; so, for example, the corner can then be ridden as one quarter of a 15-metre circle. A few simple calculations with geometry show that the corner must therefore be begun at a point 7.5 metres from the corner of the school, and finished 7.5 metres along the next turning. Much further up the scale, Grand Prix horses are asked to perform corners that are only one quarter of a 6-metre circle, or volte. However, no young horse would ever be expected to maintain his balance, carriage, pace, and elasticity on a 6-metre circle.

Once correctly executed circles, straight lines, and corners have been installed in the horse's training routine, the next step is to begin changing the rein across the school. Initially the change of rein will have to be done by moving from one large

The Rooster as a six-year-old with Dane up, competing in a medium, and as an eleven-year-old with Jackie Bickley competing at Grand Prix

circle into another, and it is important at this stage not to change through the circle so that the turn involved is any tighter than the diameter of the circle being ridden. So, for example, if riding a 15-metre circle at one end of the school, ask the horse to leave the circle quietly at a point on it that is a tangent to the diagonal. At this point change the horse's flexion so he is aware of which way he is

going to go next, and then ask him to enter into a circle that is equivalent to the one that has just been ridden, but is on the opposite rein.

As the horse's ability advances, and he moves around the arena more easily, incorporating slightly tighter corners, you can introduce changing the rein across the diagonal of the school. This involves riding into a corner of the school, and then diagonally across the school to the opposite corner. Particularly with young horses, it is important to maintain their inside positioning across the diagonal, until nearly reaching the track at the other side. The new positioning must be introduced over about four strides, so it is fully established before then riding through the corner, and carrying on on the other rein.

TRANSITIONS

The horse should at this stage be learning to change pace. The key to riding good 'transitions' is in setting them up correctly, by simply getting the horse to gather himself up a little more, or to move on a little more; he can then be ridden smoothly from halt to walk, walk to trot, and to canter, and the other way round, through the downward transitions, without his degree of balance or self-carriage altering. With a young horse, it is important that you don't ask him to perform a transition too abruptly. Take up to ten or twelve strides to prepare him fully so that when it finally comes, the transition is smooth but defined. For example, in gathering up a horse for a transition from canter to trot, take many strides to do so, until the stage is reached where the horse is likely to break into trot anyway. Then with a little use of the aids, and the voice, the horse can be brought quietly back into the trot. When moving from trot to canter, slightly accelerate the trot until the horse is ready to accept your aid, and then move up into canter.

The importance of transitions can't be understated. The horse needs to be able to go faster and slower in such a way that he increases his level of self-carriage and the engagement of the hindquarters, and as a result becomes lighter in the forehand. Ideally the contact throughout the transitions should be of an even weight, and comfortable for both horse and rider. Some horses, however, may back off the hand and completely

(Left and above) Two excellent examples of 'four square'

(Opposite above) An excellent example of a horse maintaining his balance and composure through a 6m corner: Frances Hooper and Park Royal at Badminton in 1995, and a less refined example (below)

(Below) This horse is showing attentiveness and engagement during a half-halt

reject the contact, whilst others will rush against the rein and be far too heavy. The transitions may be used to improve the horse's general way of going, as may half-halts, which will be discussed later. If the horse does not respond willingly to your asking him to make a transition, you may have to use a slightly firmer hand, leg, or back aid, not to make him do as you want, but to make him respect the fact that you are actually asking him to do something at all.

This brings to light the differentiation between the aids and a correction. The aids should always be applied very lightly. The correction, however, may have to be a little firmer in its application, not to make the horse do the transition, or whatever it was you asked him to do, but to make him listen to you, so that when you then apply the aid again, he actually responds in the way that you wanted him to do in the first place. It is terribly important then to call the horse to your attention to make him listen to lighter aids, and not to increase the weight of your aids, which in the long run will make him more unresponsive.

(Above) Bright Spark showing a good transition up into extended trot

(Below) This horse has just come out of the short side in counter canter, and is showing an excellent transition in to extended canter

• *The problem with horses is that they can't read; they are also living creatures, and have a mind of their own. Whilst they can be taught to respond to and obey our commands, they can't be made to, and quite often problems can occur, especially in the training of a young horse, which may become confused, or misunderstand what he is being asked to do. The following basic problems have therefore been devised to help the rider in training the horse by preparing him for what can go wrong, and suggesting how he might correct it.* •

What if the horse falls in on, or out of, the circle?

This is a common problem which all horses seem to show at one time or another, either tending to drift towards the centre of the circle, or trying to continue down the outside of the school and not turning at all.

If the horse falls in, I find it is generally easiest to correct this problem by first of all checking that the criteria of the horse going forwards with a rhythm and a shape are being correctly adhered to; usually the answer to the problem lies in this alone. However, if the horse persists in this evasion it can be very useful to send him on more quickly and to take the outside hand wide and lead the horse to the outside of the circle, at the same time as maintaining his bend, pushing outwards with the inside leg, and treading firmly on the outside stirrup in such a way as to influence the horse with your bodyweight. It is important to

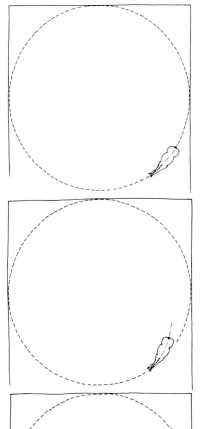

Riding a 20m circle (from top to bottom): correctly executed; the quarters falling in; the quarters falling out

exaggerate the aid sufficiently so it is clear what you want, and to take the horse past the point on the circle from which he deviated. Then it is a simple matter of allowing him to return to the circle shape.

A more difficult problem is the horse that falls out of the circle, or

even bluntly refuses to be taken from the long side onto the circle. If unchecked this can lead to the horse napping away from the direction that he has been asked to turn in. As with all these problems they are best corrected by not allowing them to begin. Should the problem exist however, I find it useful yet again to ride more accurately forwards, keeping my hands wider apart than I would normally, and guiding the horse with an open and leading inside hand, and a bit of bodyweight pressing into the inside stirrup, back to the inside of the circle – I would ask him to perform a slightly smaller circle than previously, and only then allow him to resume a normal circle size.

What if his loses his bend?

One often sees riders struggling to keep their horse on a specific circle size and only achieving this at the expense of the horse's flexion and bend: however, the horse cannot be performing a circle if he is not looking in the direction he is going. Here the open hand can really be useful, in that the outside hand can be taken to the outside with more exaggeration thus leading the horse out on the circle, with the inside leg directing the horse's quarters also to the outside of the circle; at the same time as these aids (inside leg, outside rein and bodyweight) the inside hand can keep the head to the inside of the circle thus maintaining the bend required. As a result the horse will travel somewhat sideways around the circle and it will be easier for the rider to establish a bend to the inside in his ribcage. When the horse accepts this, he can then be allowed, by riding him actively forwards, to come back more truly onto the circle shape, but this time with the correct bend. This should be repeated as many times as is necessary to get the message through to the horse until he is able to understand and perform what is required of him.

As always, the aids should not become rough, but should be firm enough to exert an influence on the horse, and the rider should be very quick to reward the horse by easing the pressure of the aids as soon as the horse reponds correctly. I often tell my students to check the bend visually by glancing briefly at the horse's inside ear and then the point of his inside hip: this will enable them to check whether the bend is uniform throughout the horse's length as it should be; and they will also then be sure that the feel they are developing is the correct feel.

What if my horse loses his rhythm?

In this case the first thing to do is to make sure that the horse is moving actively forwards, and above all that he is sound. Mostly, rhythm falters due to the lack of an active swinging stride. Once this is established or re-established the rider can then focus upon the horse's footfall and follow a beat which will enable him to find a tempo which suits him and the horse.

What if my horse doesn't follow a consistent size of corner?

Errors in riding corners are usually

This diagram shows the relative sizes and positions of the corners within the arena

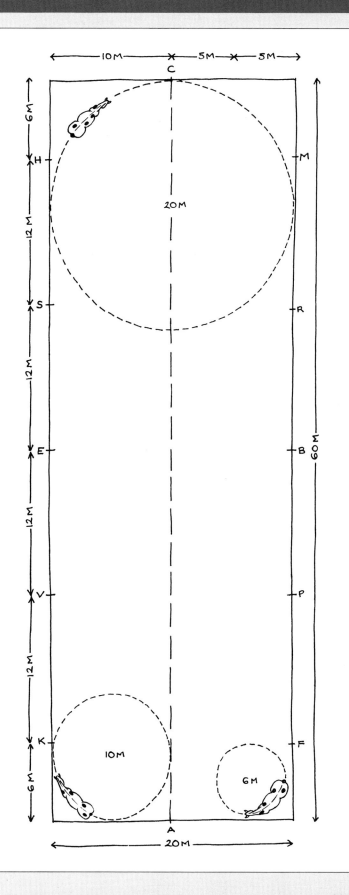

due to the fact that the rider does not treat the corner as a quarter of a circle, but rather as a right-angled turn. With novice horses, it is quite sufficient to ride a corner that is a quarter of a 20 or 15-metre circle. A few moments should be spent working out the geometry of a turn, that is to say, where the centre of the circle should be should the corner be continued, and therefore at what point on the track the horse should begin and finish the circle. For example a corner whose continuation would produce a 15-metre circle would entail the rider leaving the track at a point 7.5 metres from the corner of the school, in other words 1.5 metres before the corner marker. This may sound complicated, but with a little planning the rider will then know at exactly what point to leave the track and rejoin it again, and that will be sufficient to give an even curve through the corner. Too small a corner will result in the horse finding it difficult to maintain his balance, and he will not only lose his rhythm but inevitably his desire to go forwards, too.

What if my horse slows down before each corner?

This is again most probably due to the fact that the horse has been ridden through the corner in such a way that he has been unable to maintain his impulsion, normally by the corner being too tight. The answer will often be found in riding a much larger corner, and initially sending the horse on down the long side and then through the corner at a faster speed until he realises that he can maintain his balance on the turn. It is probably better to exaggerate the correction

by going on slightly too large a corner at slightly too great a rate for a couple of attempts before returning to a revised corner size and speed. Obviously any of these corrections should be tempered by common sense, but as is usual, most riding problems are better remedied by riding forwards than by backing off.

What if my horse has difficulty in keeping straight?

If you can successfully ride the horse forwards with a rhythm and an outline in such a way that he can keep his balance, any tendency to deviate from going 'straight' can usually be corrected by riding slightly more forwards and at the same time asking for a degree of shoulder-in. The amount of shoulder-in required should be in proportion to the amount of crookedness the horse is exhibiting. However, although riding a forwards shoulder-in will correct most of these problems, the best solution to crookedness is not to allow the horse to become too crooked in the first place. Many horses will be fairly straight on the short side of the arena, only for their crookedness to increase markedly down the long side of the arena, particularly in canter. Rather than try to straighten the horse once he is on the long side it is usually easier to prepare him to remain straight by riding him in shoulder-in *before* the corner and maintaining it for as long as necessary down the long side. Whatever the correction, it must be performed thinking from the quarters through to the head, rather than the head through to the quarters. In other words, make sure that the quarters are in the right

place, then the shoulder, and then the head, rather than trying to correct the head position in the hope that the rest will come into line, because it won't. If the horse falls in off the track, which is another common problem, the first consideration should be that he accepts the aids, and only then place him correctly on the track. It is a mistake to try and hold him on the track by any means, and not to correct his way of going.

What if my horse hollows and/or leans on the rein?

Again you have to go back to the basic principles already discussed: of riding the horse obediently forwards with an even rhythm. Once you have established these it will be much easier to correct his outline. Indicating the direction and circle size with the outside rein, the head should be positioned to the inside at the same time as the horse is ridden actively forwards onto the circle. This combined with transitions, halts, and above all patience, will eventually bring the horse back into the correct outline. Some horses that blatantly ignore the rein and abuse the rider's hands would have to be firmly corrected, possibly involving them being placed back on the lunge. But remember the *aids* should be light, even if the correction may have to be more positive; the intention should be that the horse is taught to listen to a light touch, and not made to go round by heavy reins and strong legs. It is important that the rider always distinguishes clearly between the ideal aid and the necessary correction, with the goal always being to achieve lightness and harmony.

4

ADVANCING SELF-CARRIAGE

THE HALF-HALT

The aim of the half-halt is to cause the horse to shift his weight onto his quarters, by increasing the flexion and understepping of the hind legs, thus improving the balance by lightening the forehand. This should be achieved by a co-ordinated but hardly visible action of the seat, leg and hands.

The half-halt is another vital part of the horse's training, but should only be introduced when he is able to carry himself in a balanced way with the rider on his back, and able to execute simple transitions between the paces. It took me a long time when I began riding to understand what was meant by the term 'half-halt'. I could find no clear explanation and had to work out the meaning for myself. There are many definitions of the half-halt, but none of them provides a clear explanation as to what it actually is. It often appears from the written word that it involves a jerking of the horse back onto its hind legs in a rather hurried manner. Whilst this is almost certainly not probably the intention of the many people who have written about half-halts, it has certainly been read as such by many riders and thus one sees very abrupt and harsh half-halts being applied to the horse. If you pull a horse onto his hocks, assuming that he is willing enough to allow you to do this, you will only cause him damage and pain in the hocks or back.

As far as I am concerned, the way in which 'half-halt' has been translated from the German has caused some of the biggest misconceptions that we have had in the past in the dressage world. The German word for it is *parade*, and as with the French word, *descent de main*, neither quite

explains fully what is required of the movement. For me, the half-halt is actually more of a partial transition, and the way in which each half-halt is performed may vary from the next one.

What we are actually trying to achieve from the use of the half-halt is to get the horse more actively engaged, so that he steps underneath himself with his hind legs, thus causing his croup to lower, and allowing the forehand to lighten so that the head and neck can be raised and arched until the poll becomes the highest point. If you do a very progressive transition from trot to walk, in that you reduce the speed of the trot, and actually shorten the trot strides, the horse should eventually lower his quarters, and then come down into walk. So, if you collect the horse up for this transition, in a way similar to that just explained, and having proceeded about half-way towards it, then speed the horse back up again to his previous stride and energy level, you will have performed an elementary form of the half-halt.

To me, there is no use in performing the half-halt unless you have actually taught the horse what you mean. By this I am saying that there is no use in trying to half-halt the novice horse as you would the Grand Prix horse: at the highest levels, the half-halt happens almost as soon as the rider thinks of it; with the novice horse it will probably take ten to twelve strides for him to understand that he is required not just to slow down, but to actually step up to the bridle.

A successful half-halt relies on the correct application of the aids. Ask firstly with your seat, followed by your leg, and then your hand. Hanging on to the front end, and thereby inhibiting the movement of the horse, must be avoided. A simple but useful exercise for teaching the half-halt is progressively to shorten, and shorten the stride, and then gradually to increase and stretch the stride, until the horse gets the idea of moving freely between this transition. By adjusting the stride within the horse's pace he will become accustomed to collecting himself and to lowering his quarters, to shortening the stride, and then gradually moving forwards. The emphasis here must be placed upon gradual, rather than immediate variances within the pace.

You may find that the horse 'blocks' half-way through your aid for the half-halt, at which point you have a decision to make, in that you can either back off, or persist firmly until the horse responds to what you are asking of him. Either of these solutions will be the correct one, if applied at the correct moments, and when they are needed will be learned from experience by the rider.

As the horse progresses in his training he will be expected to perform the half-halt with more immediacy upon your request. For a horse working at elementary level, the half-halt can be performed over perhaps six to eight strides. By the time advanced level is reached, the horse will be expected to come together, sit and lower in the same proportion as he is asked by the rider's aids. However, when loosening up a horse, whatever level he is working at, it can often be very beneficial to take time to practise the long half-halts, so the horse has to lengthen and shorten his stride as required, and is made to listen to the aids; for me, the half-halt is really a test of the horse's willingness to accept the rider's aids.

In learning how to ride the half-halt, it may help to imagine the horse as a concertina, in that what you are aiming to do is squeeze the horse together, and then open him out again. If you squeeze too quickly, you will undermine what you are trying to achieve because you will lose all impulsion, but on the other hand if you are too slow to demand the half-halt, you most likely won't achieve the result you are after. The key to riding good half-halts therefore lies in achieving the balance necessary in applying the aids in order for the horse to achieve a higher level of collection.

The teaching of the half-halt is probably one of the most important elements in training the horse. Its main importance lies in its use to prepare the horse for other movements, since in effect it causes him to be more collected, with a high level of self-carriage, and his hocks underneath him. However, as with all the movements that you want the horse to perform, you must be sure that you actually *teach* him what to do, before you expect him to do it in response to your normal aids, to avoid confusion, and to avoid any possible resistances by the horse.

COLLECTION

The aim of collection is to improve the self-carriage of the horse, particularly as this will have been disturbed by the addition of the rider's weight. This has to be achieved by causing the horse to lower his quarters by engaging the hind leg: that is to say, the degree of flexion and understep of the hind leg has to be increased.

Having developed the ability of the horse so he can perform simple transitions, and also his degree of self-carriage to the level required to achieve these easily, it is now necessary to ask him to perform certain movements. The horse should have established his paces and balance in such a way that he can carry himself and his rider with ease: what then becomes the test of his way of going is actually his ability to perform various school movements. Without any of this classical underpinning – that is if the horse does not have these basics established – he will merely be performing simple tricks that can be taught to any amenable horse. What makes the movements 'classical' in identity is the nature of the basic underlying training; and this brings to light the point of collection.

Collection is a very widely banded term and has various meanings to different people. For me, collection is quite simply a state of readiness. If you have a novice horse and he is ready to perform a movement for you in that he is alert, balanced and on the aids, this readiness, coupled with his ability to perform the movement with ease, can actually be classified as a collected state for his stage of training. A Grand Prix horse will obviously be asked to perform much more difficult tasks. These movements or tasks, be they of a novice or a Grand Prix horse, are really the proof that the basic training is soundly established; the proof that the horse has achieved a certain level of carriage and balance and therefore that he has achieved sufficient

These three pictures indicate the improved carriage and engagement resulting from increasing levels of collection being achieved

(Left) Novice pony; (Above) Seven-year-old advanced gelding; (Below) Bright Spark in his first Prix St Georges

degree of collection for his level of training.

The degree of collection that would be required in the novice horse is obviously nowhere near the same degree as that required in the Grand Prix horse. Nonetheless it is important to realise that each horse is collected *in his own way*: certainly in dressage tests at a lower level, when only a small degree of collection is required, there seems to be an awful lot of confusion, and judges and riders are often heard saying that the horses were either too collected, or not collected enough. Really it may be wiser for them to take a more simplistic view of collection, this being the readiness of the horse to perform the movements with willingness and ease: if he can perform all the movements without any hindrance to his basic way of going, maintaining obedience, forward movement and rhythmical outline in such a way that he has self-carriage and balance, then in my opinion he is collected enough.

THE DOUBLE BRIDLE

It is at this stage that one might consider introducing the horse to the double bridle. Quite simply it contains two bits that are placed in the horse's mouth, and which offer the rider maximum influence and control over the horse's head and neck position. It is a very severe bitting arrangement, and should only be put into a horse's mouth when he has had a thorough training in the snaffle. Having said this, I know of many riders who have insisted on training their horses only in a double bridle. In experienced hands this does not cause a problem if it is done properly. Equally, there are some horses which are much more comfortable in a double bridle than in a snaffle, probably due to the fact that they feel more secure because of the greater control the rider has over them, allowing them to find their balance more easily. It would therefore be wise to ride such horses mostly in a double in order to persuade the best possible work out of them.

Initially, I fit the double bridle in the stable myself, trying to make sure that everything is as comfortable as possible for the horse. Make sure that the position of the bridoon bit is more or less

Correctly fitted double bridle (top), and snaffle bridle

identical to that of the snaffle and that the curb bit is resting just below this. The bars of the curb should in no way interfere with the horse's teeth by being too low, and similarly, the bridoon should not be so high as to interfere with the molars. More often than not, if a horse is uncomfortable with a double, it is due to incorrect fitting, and often the bits are causing discomfort in the horse's mouth by being either too high or too low. The noseband I like to do up comfortably and securely, making sure that it isn't too tight, but fits snugly and is fairly high up on the horse's face so that it sits just

This horse is going very kindly in a double bridle for the first time

under the projecting cheekbones of the horse's face.

The curb chain should be done up in such a way that the arms of the curb can rotate through approximately forty-five degrees before the chain becomes taut. This gives the horse plenty of room to feel the bit, but without feeling the pressure of the curb the whole time. The chain should lie flat and even, and behind the horse's chin groove, and should be fixed to the bits in such a way that there are no edges projecting into the horse's mouth. A simple thing to watch out for is that the curb hooks are connected to the curb bit in such a way that they don't hook into, or interfere with, the cheek-pieces of the bridoon. In my experience, it is not uncommon to see these hooks actually projecting

into the holes of the mouthpiece where the ring runs through, thereby locking up the bit – a most unsatisfactory practice.

It is wise to let the horse feel the action of the reins whilst he is still standing in the stable. You can cause him to flex using the bridoon before very gently taking up the curb rein. At first only apply a very small amount of pressure on the reins. If the horse shows no obvious signs of tension or resistance, then gradually increase the pressure a little more until he can fully feel the action of the curb on his mouth and head. By doing this, the horse encounters this pressure in a situation in which he is unlikely to get too tense or worried. If the first time that he feels the curb rein is when the rider is on him, then problems may be encountered.

When the horse is first ridden with the double bridle on, ride him with initially hardly any contact on the curb rein at all, just enough to stop the reins looping too much; keep the majority of the contact with the bridoon rein. Ride the horse a little more actively forwards than you might otherwise, just as a precaution in case he starts backing off the bits. Let the horse then feel the pressure of the curb rein gradually, by taking it up very gently. Always, even at this stage, the main contact should be via the bridoon rein, with the curb rein acting very much as an auxiliary aid. Eventually you may find that the horse will accept the rein quite comfortably and without getting upset, though at this stage it depends on the individual horse as to how much rein contact is established with each of the bits. In an ideal world, the horse should always be worked off the bridoon, the curb being the back-up. The bridoon is the main way of pushing the horse up into the bridle, whilst the function of the curb bit is to aid the arching and positioning of the horse's head and neck to give him a greater degree of lightness in his forehand.

COUNTER-CANTER

The aim of counter-canter is to cause the horse to canter on the wrong lead, whilst maintaining his carriage, including the correct flexion (towards the leading leg). When used correctly, the counter-canter is a very good method of suppling and loosening the horse.

Counter-canter is something I tend to teach my horses fairly early on in their training because I find that it is not a very difficult movement for them to learn; moreover, it is very beneficial in terms of improving their general balance and carriage.

In my opinion, the biggest problem with the counter-canter is the mental attitude of the rider. All that you are doing is asking the horse to canter on a certain leg, but on the opposite rein to that which you would normally be on if you were cantering on that leg. If his canter is balanced and he can perform relatively small circles and turns – for example, he should be able to perform a 15-metre circle in canter without any loss of balance – then the horse can begin to be taught to counter-canter. The horse should also be able to execute simple transitions from walk to canter and trot to canter, in order to make the teaching of counter-canter easier.

There are several ways in which counter-canter can be taught. The one I favour is to travel down the long side in true canter, then to ride a small circle of between 10 and 15 metres upon reaching the end of the long side. Continue the circle round until you are on a line that will return you directly back to the track; as you approach the track, re-emphasise the canter aids whilst also pushing the horse on to make sure that he doesn't break. Most horses will do this without fighting the rider too much. However, the problem comes as the rider begins to turn the corner to rejoin the long side of the school; at this point many horses will initially find it difficult to remain on the outside lead. It is therefore wise to make the turn as shallow as possible by returning to the track approximately half-way along the long side; it is also advisable to begin a large half-circle loop immediately so that you are not faced with riding through the corners of the school in counter-canter at this stage.

In counter-canter it is very important that you don't hang on to the inside rein. For example, if you are cantering on the right lead in counter-canter, you will have to do a left turn, and it is therefore very important that the horse has learned to move up into the left rein, keeping his balance whilst he does this. If the rider grabs the inside rein at this stage, then the horse will tend to lie on that rein and will either fall out of the canter into trot, or possibly by losing his balance, will change onto the left leg to regain his lost balance. In either case,

the most likely result is that the horse will lose his confidence because he is finding it difficult to maintain his balance.

It is therefore very important to push the horse up into the outside rein; so with the canter on the right lead, you must push the horse up into the left rein. On the long side, practise giving and retaking the right rein. Obviously this rein must not be totally abandoned, and a small amount of contact should be kept on it the majority of the time. I often try to get the horse to counter-flex slightly so that he bends against the canter lead, which stops his neck stiffening on the left-hand side whilst also pushing him forwards. If I am riding through the turn and the horse starts to stiffen and to falter in the canter, I will obviously give the reins away as much as I can to correct this, and will ride him quickly forwards. Don't in any way try to hold the horse up in front with the use of the reins; if he falls on his nose a little bit or loses his balance, then this is his problem, so to speak – simply repeat the canter strike-off until he is able to keep his balance.

It is important not to do too much counter-canter in the early stages, but merely a sufficient amount for the horse to be able to travel through the half circle already discussed. On reaching the opposite long side, bring him back into trot or walk, have a short break and then repeat the movement. In the early stages I will also make sure that I start the counter-canter exercise by being on the correct lead for whichever rein I am travelling on, before changing the rein and introducing counter-canter.

Once the horse can do this exercise with relative ease, you can start to ask him to go a little more through the corners, and to maintain counter-canter for longer. Another useful exercise is to bring the horse back to walk after the corner, and then to canter him again on the outside lead so that he is back in counter-canter before going through the next corner. This can be particularly useful for horses that tend to rush away in counter-canter. Don't be too abrupt in bringing them back to walk, as you want them to be able to re-establish their balance through the transition and the walk paces that follow; then reintroduce the canter which as a result will enjoy a new degree of carriage and collection, allowing them to move smoothly through the corner.

When the horse can basically maintain his

(Above and right) Bright Spark showing good balance in a counter-canter circle on the left lead

balance, I will use the simple transitions from canter to walk and walk to canter repeatedly at different places around the school and progressively take the horse deeper into the corners so that he is able to maintain his balance on a much tighter counter-canter turn. Under no circumstances must the horse be allowed to fall out of the canter, or to lean on the rider's hands. If he does, he must be taken back a couple of stages in his training, with the balance being re-established in his normal canter, before counter-canter is repeated. Trying to force a horse into counter-canter will only result in at best the rider hanging on to the horse through the corners, rather than the horse learning to maintain his own balance by adding more weight to his hind legs.

Once all this has been achieved, you can change the rein and also make changes of lead, through either a flying change, or a simple change, depending on whether the horse has learned the movements or not. The horse can be taught to canter first on one lead and then on the other. Put him through various different turns and shapes in counter-canter until his confidence is enough to allow him to maintain counter-canter through any turn around the arena which the rider asks of him. In the current FEI Prix St Georges test, the horse is actually required to counter-canter through a half

10-metre circle. It is only a horse that can really keep his balance in counter-canter that is going to be able to perform this movement well and fulfil the requirements of the test.

Once the horse is fully established in counter-canter, then I use it regularly to improve his balance and to teach him how to carry himself with greater ease. In this respect it can be a very useful tool to improve many other movements, as well as the basic way of going of the horse.

THE REIN-BACK

The rein-back is a two-time movement whereby the horse maintains his desire to move forwards, whilst moving backwards. The legs should move in diagonal pairs, and the horse should move in a straight line without any tendency to drag the feet. The outline and self-carriage should be maintained.

The rein-back is a movement in which the horse is required to take strides backwards upon the rider's demands. The steps should be of even height, regular and should be taken in diagonal pairs. The movement has many uses, including that of impressing obedience on certain horses. It is also part of a confidence-gaining step for the horse, because once he can do it and learns to trust you, you will find that his confidence improves in many of the other movements.

I find the best way to teach the rein-back is to begin by introducing it when the horse is coming out of his stable. Take the horse into a clear area and simply push him back with your hand on his shoulder, keeping a little bit of contact on the reins. Some horses take to this exercise like a duck to water, whilst others thoroughly resent being pushed back with any contact of the rein. If the horse really resists, put a foot against one of his front hooves and tread lightly on it, which should encourage him to move back. As a last resort, touch him gently on the leg or shoulder with a schooling whip until he responds. When you are performing the finished movement on the horse, the rein contact should be extremely light, and almost imperceptible aids should be given when you ask for it. These aids should consist of seat, leg and bodyweight.

However, initially the idea should be put into the horse's head that he should step back on command by using this exercise of pushing him back from the ground. Make use of your voice as an aid, too, encouraging the horse by actually telling him to go 'back'. When reining back for the first few times whilst actually on the horse's back, you may have to use your hands as a slightly stronger aid; more so than you would wish to use them when he has learned the movement. This is why I favour teaching the horse to go back from the ground first of all, so that when you come to actually riding the movement mounted, your hand aids don't have to be quite so strong – this could quite possibly lead to resistance from the horse, who may either run back or stand up to avoid your rein contact. It is therefore always best to ask for small steps backwards initially, and not to fuss over their regularity; just be pleased that he obeys your aids and does actually travel backwards.

Having established this on the horse's back, you can then start to be a little more correct in your approach to the rein-back. Firstly, push the horse up into a very square halt with his hocks engaged and underneath his body. His neck should be raised and arched so that he is lightly on the bit. My initial move now would be to go forwards rather than backwards because the idea of the rein-back is that although the horse is taking steps that are in reverse, the feeling should be that he is stepping forwards to the hands. This exercise of halting and then moving forwards in walk should be repeated two or three times until the horse is really listening to the rider. When the horse is feeling really responsive, halt again, put your legs on, and as he goes to take a forward step, restrain him with your hands very slightly to encourage him to move backwards. If he blocks against the rein, give and retake until he releases, then continue asking him back as before. As soon as he responds, pat him, walk forwards and position him for another attempt. By teaching the horse in this way, I find that most will master the rein-back in a very short period of time.

This is where the classical requirements of dressage should be employed, in that the horse should not just walk backwards, but should walk up into the bridle as the rider closes his legs and lifts his seat slightly; the forward steps should be translated into ones which move upwards and backwards. Initially the rider should never ask the horse to take too large a stride backwards, and short controlled strides are more desirable; but as the horse grows in confidence you will find that he will begin to step back more boldly.

Don't worry if, to begin with, your horse steps back crookedly. For example, his quarters may well swing to one side or the other – but don't punish him for this, as long as he is offering you the basic backward steps. It is only a matter of control and influence in the later stages of training to make the horse step back straight.

Once your horse moves backwards off the legs with as little rein aid as possible, you can then start to pay more attention to both the height and straightness of the steps. Initially ask the horse to rein back straight, not by hanging on to one rein or the other, but by subtle controlling of the steps. If he moves off crookedly to one side, draw your leg on that side slightly further back than you would normally apply it, and feel the rein on that same side. Don't use your leg harshly, but just keep it in position. If the horse continues to be crooked, apply a small amount of pressure with your leg until he is travelling back straight. It is very important that you don't hang on to the reins when the horse tries to move crookedly. He should move straight because he feels confident to take an even stride backwards without any undue pressure upon him.

Some horses take several crooked strides before they understand that your leg which is back is actually directing them in a straight line. As the rider, make sure you don't become impatient and force the horse into a straight line. If, for example, the horse's quarters were curved to the right and he subsequently stepped back in this direction, put your right leg back and feel both reins; feel the right a little more than the left, and ask him ever so gently as he moves back, to straighten his stride. Don't worry if you find that you are having to take a fairly large number of strides backwards in order to correct the horse's crookedness. This causes no problem as long as you don't force the horse backwards onto his hocks and rush him back, in which case he may well panic.

In summary, the rein-back should really be a translation of your forward pushing aids, so that even though the horse is striding backwards, he should feel exactly the same as he does when he is striding forwards. Some horses can perform the movement with ease in the early stages of their training, whilst others can be really worried by it, therefore taking longer to build up their confidence; but for each horse the basic principles of practising the movement are the same.

(Right) Mester showing self-carriage in rein-back

(Below) Here I am pushing Mester back up into the bridle to correct an evasive overbend

A good counter-canter has its base in a well-prepared and balanced collected canter: Kirsty Mepham and Red Garth at Royal Windsor

then be able to correct into a true canter on the other lead. To prevent such an incident happening, make sure that the horse is carrying himself sufficiently before you proceed further and try to make the counter-canter more advanced. With horses that really rush away and get confused about counter-canter, I find it very useful to bring the horse back into walk from the canter, and then to canter on again, and to do this repeatedly. By doing lots of these transitions the horse will learn to find his balance gradually, as he will only have a short amount of counter-canter to do before he is able to walk and re-establish his balance; he is then better prepared to strike off into counter-canter again.

In this fashion you can progress your way through the corners as the horse learns to find his balance more (the corners obviously being the most difficult area of the school in which to maintain counter-canter), and eventually you should be able to maintain counter-canter on even the smallest of turns and circles.

What if my horse repeatedly changes legs when he is asked to counter-canter?

If a horse changes legs in counter-canter, the change will probably happen more often than not in front, rather than behind, unless the horse is already established at executing flying changes; if he persists in doing this he must be made more alert to the aids in general before proceeding any further. He must then be set up correctly, and made to go through the counter-canter turns by careful adjustment of his balance.

What if my horse fails to maintain the canter when I am practising counter-canter?

This is one of the most common problems with counter-canter. An inexperienced horse is more than likely to stumble or fall out of the canter, either into a trot, or into a disunited canter, which he may

5

DEVELOPING FLEXIBILITY
Introducing Extensions and Lateral Work

Transitions are used either to change between the paces or to change the speed within a pace. The aim is that these transitions should occur rapidly but show no hint of abruptness. The pace must remain regular at all times throughout the transition, with the horse maintaining his self-carriage, whilst calmly and willingly accepting the rider's aids.

Having reached the stage of training with your horse whereby he is established in the execution of circles and straight lines, and can carry out simple transitions with ease, as well as responding effectively to the rider's half-halt aid, he can then be asked for more immediate transitions and introduced to lateral work. This will require the horse to be more attentive and alert to the rider's aids and to respond with more immediacy. This does not mean that his reactions must be abrupt, but rather that he is simply more 'on the aids'.

At this stage the horse should be asked to increase, through the use of the half-halt, his degree of collection; this might otherwise be expressed as the engagement and lowering of his hindquarters which results in the lightening and raising of his forehand, so that the poll is drawn up to the highest point. This state of collection will in turn enable the horse to move forwards by the enhanced lowering and pushing of his hind legs, giving him the power to move into the extended paces. Again, these transitions should in no way be rushed, or abrupt, and should be easy for the horse to perform.

DEVELOPMENT OF TRANSITIONS AND MEDIUM AND EXTENDED PACES

The aim is to develop the training so that in the medium work, when the horse is asked to go forwards with a reasonably extended stride, he should exhibit a lot of energetic impulsion as a result of pushing from his quarters. His outline should remain rounded, although not as round as in collected trot, and his head should be slightly more in front of the vertical. In extension, he should cover as much ground with each stride as possible, showing an enormous amount of impulsion, whilst remaining calm. He should maintain a light contact and a good balance. His frame should also lengthen to permit the lengthening of the stride.

In all the transitions and movements that the horse performs and as they increase in difficulty, he requires a concomitant degree of collection. The same degree of collection is required to perform the piaffe, as is required to perform the extended trot, contrary to what may otherwise by assumed. To perform well the horse has to be able to execute all the required movements with the maximum of ease, and he must therefore have an engagement of the hindquarters to the extent where he can truly carry a greater degree of weight on his hind legs.

It is this shifting of weight onto the hindquarters, combined with the pushing and thrusting, that will give the medium and extended trots their reach and elegance. In the same way a similar action of the hindquarters will give the piaffe swing and cadence, with a certain degree of increased suspension. What I am really trying to highlight here is therefore a different manifestation of exactly the same thing, that being *engagement*.

The engagement of the horse also depends quite significantly on his ability to perform transitions well, which is why these movements are referred to by so many trainers as the life-blood of the training of the horse. If the horse cannot execute transitions within the paces, he will fail later on in his training in his ability to engage his hindquarters sufficiently. The transitions can also be considered as the 'weight training' part of the development of the horse: in the short term they make the horse better able to increase the level of bend and self-carriage, whilst maintaining the cadence of his stride, because the contraction of the muscles necessitated in performing them results in the horse's physique being able to compress itself more easily, and this in turn results in a greater degree of carriage. In the long term, the strength of the horse's physical musculature will of course be increased through the repeated performance of many transitions.

When performing these transitions, the rider should set himself in his mind a certain number of strides in which to collect the horse and execute the actual transition. For example, in the trot to halt transition, it is sensible to think of allowing the horse approximately eight to ten strides to move from a balanced trot to a balanced halt. When he is able to do this transition with ease, the number of strides you allow him to execute the transition can progressively be reduced.

It must be taken into account that there is no such thing as an instant transition from one pace to another. No matter how quickly the horse performs the transition, it will take a certain amount of time to complete, be this only a few seconds, or fractions of a second. What must be aimed for is to execute the transition in as short a time as is reasonable to expect the horse to perform at his stage of training. He must never be pressured to perform *above* his capabilities, but on the other hand can always be asked to perform to the *extent* of his capabilities. In this way his abilities will be stretched to a point at which he is still confident, and this will teach him not only to do what you ask

of him, but also to meet your requirements with ease.

Depending on the ability of the individual horse, it can take between a few days and several weeks to make the transitions from, for example, medium trot to collected trot and then to halt. Each horse will have his own time-span in which he is capable of executing these transitions, and it is the rider's responsibility to discover what this length of time is. The horse should only be pushed to the limit of his abilities for a very short time because otherwise his muscles will become too fatigued to carry on with the particular movement or exercise. However, exercising the muscles in short bursts can actually develop his abilities, making him capable of sustaining this strain for longer in the future.

An important point to take into account is that you can reduce the ignorance of a horse by correct and insistent training, but you can't reduce his fatigue. Any attempt to teach a tired horse will be totally worthless, and may even cause more damage than good. Moreover the fatigue of the horse may not only be physical, but also mental, especially in the case of young horses who will most likely only be capable of short periods of concentration. It must be remembered, as I have already said, that horses are living creatures, and their mental attitude has to be taken into consideration. If the horse thinks he can't do something he will defend himself against being asked to do it; and if, on the other hand, he thinks he can do it, there is no possible reason why he should not.

When you practise transitions from one pace to another, or within the paces – for example, from medium to collected and collected to medium – it is important that you allow the horse time to think about what is required of him, as well as the time to offer you his maximum effort. Again, I feel it necessary to stress the fact that it should be the rider and the horse working together, not against each other. In the real world, all riders are going to be too greedy in what they ask of their horse at one time or another. The ideal situation whereby the rider asks the horse something to which he responds immediately and in the correct way does not occur very frequently for most riders.

Five-year-old Virtu and Dane preparing for an extended trot

As a rider, you must be prepared to admit when you have made an error, to learn from your mistake, and then try not to repeat it again. Situations will invariably occur when you work the horse far too long and hard, and it is the foolish rider who denies that he has done this, or does not try to make amends once he has done it; thus if you make the mistake of over-working a horse on one day, then you must make it up to him the next by relaxing him, and demanding less of him and allowing him to relax in his work.

When the rider asks a more immediate transition from the horse, this does not necessarily mean that the transition has to be instantaneous to the aids. It is much nicer to see a horse settling into, for example, a very balanced halt over a couple of steps, than it is to see him being hauled back into the halt without adequate preparation for the transition; like this the transition can barely be termed as a 'halt', but rather a 'stop'. For me, the halt should exhibit engagement, balance and

carriage, as with all other transitions, and if the horse needs a fairly lengthy period of time to make the transition smoothly, then his abilities should be developed until he *can* execute it with the same ease and quality within a shorter space of time.

In all the transitions, the basic ability of the horse to think forwards and remain forwards, even at the halt, and his ability to maintain his rhythm and shape, will lead to his being able to stay in balance. Thus the key to executing smooth transitions is keeping the horse in balance. To the observer, the transitions must look as if they occur naturally; there should be no obvious effort made by the rider to get the horse to perform – the aids should be almost imperceptible. With time and training, the horse's acceptance of the aids can become so acute that it really doesn't look as if the rider is having to do anything at all. When this stage is reached, you have achieved a very high level of riding and training with your horse.

The preparation required to perform upward

Bright Spark beginning to collect after an extended canter. He has become a little short in the neck here

(Left) Bright Spark and Daniel in medium trot

transitions, such as from collected trot into the medium or extended trot, is the same as that required for the highly collected piaffe and passage. The horse must be really collected and up onto his hocks, so that at that moment he is at the maximum of his ability to carry as much weight as he possibly can on his hind legs – although this state of collection should in no way interfere with his basic way of going, that is, with elastic, forward-moving steps. However, the horse must be collected in such a way in order to extend, because only then is he in a good position to thrust underneath himself with his hind legs and effectively push the ground down and away behind him so that his body goes up and forwards, so enabling the length of the stride to increase.

When asking the horse to extend it is a mistake for the rider to push him at every stride, as this can make his steps choppy and may encourage him to run. By pushing at every other stride, however, the horse has the stride in between to himself, giving him the chance to sort out his balance himself and hopefully to offer you even more extension. In the initial stages of the extension, ask for it progressively, so that each step becomes a little longer. Your interference as a rider should be kept to the absolute minimum so as not to disturb the horse's carriage or balance, which once lost in the beginning stages, or even in the middle of the extension, will be hard to regain within the movement.

By riding the extensions in this way I have found that the horse is more willing to give you what you ask, because he is given a suitable period of time, depending on his abilities and level of training, within which to perform the movement. A poorer extension will be produced if the horse is pushed too quickly so that he becomes out of balance and rhythm and is forced into a way of going that is not based upon the classical guidelines. By pushing the horse onwards gradually until he reaches the level at which he is required to go, he will discover his own abilities and limitations.

Half the task of teaching the horse to extend is also teaching him how to collect or to rebalance at the end of the extension. It is not uncommon to see horses perform impressive extensions, only to fall into a heap at the other side of the school as the rider asks them to come back. Just as it may take several strides for the horse to move from a collected to an extended pace to start with, so too will it take the same number of strides, if not more, for him to collect again after the extension. When teaching the horse to extend it is therefore important that you leave enough room at the beginning and end of the long side or diagonal, so that the horse can re-establish his balance in sufficient time before attempting to turn the corner, whilst also maintaining his cadence and carriage.

Simple preparation and planning for the extensions is therefore of great importance in their teaching, and an essential part of horse and rider gaining in confidence when performing this sort of movement. If the horse rushes forwards too quickly he is quite likely to brace his back and hollow, making it very uncomfortable for the rider to sit to his movements. In the beginning of teaching the extended trot, it is important not to sit too heavily and it is therefore wise to employ rising trot. Do, however, be careful to sit very lightly on the horse's back on the down beat of the rising trot; take care not to bang in any way on the saddle, because at this stage in the horse's training his balance will be quite precarious and very easily disturbed. Riders must therefore do everything they can to allow the horse to expand his stride and then contract it – if their riding causes him discomfort he will not be willing to use his body to his full ability.

It can be useful to ask the horse to extend on a

circle of approximately 20 metres and then to change the rein slightly across the diagonal onto another circle on the other rein. This allows the rider the chance to push the horse on around the circle, increasing the amount of energy in the stride until he reaches the diagonal where he can ask for the extension easily, and then use the other circle to rebalance the horse again. Alternatively, for some

Guadeloupe and me at the final Goodwood National Championships in extended trot in the Grand Prix class

horses, it may be best to collect as much as possible on the short side, allowing them to push themselves up and over their back, before extending across the diagonal. In the extensions, it is very important that the horse's back is raised and rounded, and that there is no tendency for it to dip away, or for the hind legs to go wide or high; these are common mistakes that must be avoided.

INTRODUCING LATERAL WORK

The aim of lateral work is to make the horse more obedient to the rider; to improve his suppleness by making him more flexible and elastic as a result of the gymnastic improvement that this work will bring about; and for the same reasons to improve the balance and engagement of the quarters. Lateral work consists of leg-yielding, shoulder-in, travers, renvers and half-pass; in all but shoulder-in and leg-yielding, the horse is bent towards the direction in which he is travelling. Above all, lateral work must be a forward and sideways movement.

A lot of the preparation for lateral work has actually already been discussed in that the horse has learned to move forwards and away from the leg on the circle. With these basics established, the teaching of lateral work should not present too many difficulties. The way I like to approach the introduction of the lateral work is to re-establish the movement of the horse away from the rider's leg firstly on the circle, and then by taking the horse large a few metres away from the track of the long side of the school.

When practising this second exercise, the horse may initially tend to wander and may try to rejoin the track, or resist the rider's leg. In general, however, it doesn't take too long for him to understand what the rider is asking of him. With some horses, it may be easier to introduce the lateral work in walk, whilst other horses need the impulsion that the trot gives in order to maintain their desire to move forwards. One of the most important things in lateral work is that the horse continually maintains his desire to move forwards in a free and easy way. In the trot and the canter lateral work, he must move with the same elastic strides as he would do in a normal trot or canter. If this criterion isn't met, the best you will achieve is a horse that stumbles in the sideways crossing of his legs and is in no way adding any enthusiasm to his strides.

By carefully adjusting the horse's position in relation to the track, you can cause his quarters to move in towards the centre of the school, whilst still effectively travelling in a straight line down the long side of the school. Having established this 'leg-yielding' position, which could almost be referred to as a 'shoulder-out', then change the rein and make sure the horse can do the same work with equal ease on the other rein. When he can do this, it is time to start to establish the shoulder-in.

The way I like to establish this movement is again on the long side of the school, although, if I am having particular difficulties then I will begin on the circle. In the ideal shoulder-in, if you look at the line that you should move along, the quarters should actually stay on this line, whilst the shoulders should move to the inside. However, in most cases when you begin teaching the horse it is easier to cheat somewhat and position the quarters slightly out as opposed to the shoulders in; it is more important for him to get the message of what you want him to do, rather than producing a copybook movement, and it is for this reason that it is sometimes acceptable to move him ever-so-slightly quarters out. Note that if this is done when the horse is too close to the wall of the school, he may feel inclined to resist the action of your inside leg because he will be afraid that you are trying to push him into the wall. It is therefore important to remain a couple of metres off the track; by travelling in from the track, you allow the horse to realise that this isn't the case, thereby increasing his confidence.

The primary requirement of the shoulder-in is that the horse maintains his free forward movement. Personally, I prefer to teach it to horses in the trot, although as I have said, with horses that are having difficulties, I will ride the movement quietly in walk. The inside leg has the action of being against the girth, in the same way that you use it when riding a circle; its actual direction of action is as if it were trying to push the horse's girth gently from the inside through to the outside shoulder. The outside leg acts in conjunction with the inside leg to maintain the horse's desire to go forwards, but also to assist should the quarters start to fall too much to the outside. The outside rein maintains the bend that is suggested by the inside rein and by the rider's bodyweight.

Mester, with Victoria Simpson, is yielding to the rider's left leg as he travels along the side of the school

Some horses can be quite awkward to teach the shoulder-in to, in that they will quite happily accept the leg-yielding exercise down the long side, but as you ask them to do the shoulder-in, you can be met with quite a lot of resistance to the leg, especially on the horse's stiffer side. I find the best way to deal with this problem is to ride the horse more actively forwards and to commence asking for the correct positioning of the horse for the shoulder-in as he is already turning the corner at the beginning of the long side. To start with, be happy to accept only a small amount of angle, or sideways stepping. Whatever you do, don't make an issue out of the movement, so that the horse tenses and resists every time you come to perform it.

I feel I should reiterate here that in the beginning, I will only require a shoulder-in *position* from the horse, rather than the fully established movement. I therefore initially won't insist that the quarters stay on exactly the same track, although this will be one of the most important criteria later on; but I will be encouraged if the horse maintains his confidence in his forward movement and his attitude, so that the angle of his travel is more or less constant, his outline is even and his rhythm is maintained.

A helpful hint is not to attempt to do any lateral work for too long a period of time to start with. The angle required for shoulder-in should generally be such that the horse is on three distinct tracks: the outside hind leg must be on one track going in the required direction, the inside hind leg and outside foreleg should follow a track which is parallel to the track of the outside hind leg, and the third parallel track is made by the inside foreleg. In reality however, the number of tracks made can change slightly according to the make and shape of the horse. Some horses may need to be on slightly more than three tracks in order to perform at their maximum carriage and engagement in shoulder-in, and this consideration is something that really has to be taken into account when working each individual horse. It is pointless to have the horse on three tracks if his conformation will not allow this easily, so that the exercise results in his stiffening

Here (right) Mester is hollowing, although he has maintained the correct bend and positioning; he moves on to produce a much improved shoulder-in (far right)

*Bright Spark showing (above) insufficient angle in
shoulder-in, and (right) slightly too much
(right) Victoria on Mester performing a good shoulder-in*

and resisting; if by moving onto a slightly greater
angle the horse finds it easier to relax and loosen
his back, he will be able to perform a better quality
shoulder-in.

The shoulder-in, if correctly ridden, will become
one of the greatest tools available to you for
training any horse, but especially the dressage
horse. It can be used later in the horse's training to
correct crookedness and in the approaches to such
movements as pirouettes, or even flying changes;
and it can also be used as preparation to set the
horse up for half-passes or extensions. It is
therefore an invaluable exercise that can be used
time and time again. Because of its usefulness, the

shoulder-in should really be an integral part of the horse's training from the very beginning, even if it is only in the form of simply positioning the horse in a manner which implies the movement. At this stage, the horse should also be capable of travelling clearly on the line of the track that you have chosen.

Having established the two basic exercises of leg-yielding and shoulder-in, it is often of great use to alternate between these two movements, so the horse becomes more supple and is used to being manoeuvred from one bend and way of travelling to the other. To start with the horse may need to take several strides in order to change from one movement to the other, and if the change-over is executed too quickly it may well only serve to make him tense and possibly build up resistances. On the other hand if it is carried out too slowly it will not have the desired effect, in that it will do little to supple the horse's back and sides: moving from leg-yielding or shoulder-out to shoulder-in requires the horse to use all his muscles in his back, sides and shoulder.

When the horse is capable of moving from one lateral position to another with relative ease, the half-pass can be introduced into his training. There are many ways to approach riding the half-pass, and many of them are governed by the same principles of the horse desiring to go forwards, maintaining his rhythm and his outline. The method which I find most useful is to teach the horse travers before introducing the half-pass itself; although having said that, travers is a movement which should be practised sparingly with horses that have a tendency to swing their quarters to the inside anyway – until this is corrected it is unwise to teach them to do so even more.

TEACHING TRAVERS

Travers is a lateral movement which involves the positioning of the horse's head, neck and shoulders on the track, whilst his quarters should be pushed to the inside of the track. This results in the middle of the horse's head looking directly in front of him, so that when travelling down the long side it would be looking at the corner at the end of the school, and the positioning of the quarters to the inside would give him a bend all the way through his body from tail to poll. Most horses find it relatively

easy to perform this movement, and it can be very useful in correcting horses who tend to back off the bit because it seems to be a particular movement in which they will push forwards and take more rein contact. As with the shoulder-in, the horse should ideally be on three tracks, although again depending on the make and shape of the horse, the number of tracks actually made may be slightly more than this due to the horse performing the movement at a greater angle.

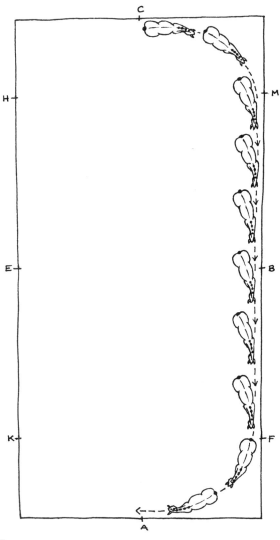

Travers

Victoria and Mester in travers left

TEACHING RENVERS

When the horse can perform travers on both reins, he can be taught renvers, which is more or less the opposite to travers in that the bend of the horse is reversed: his head and neck still look in the direction in which he is travelling, but this time the quarters stay on the track and he is bent in the opposite way to the rein he is travelling on. So for example if on the left rein, his head and neck would be bent to the right, and his forehand should travel along the track 2 metres in parallel to the track of the long side, with his quarters pushed to

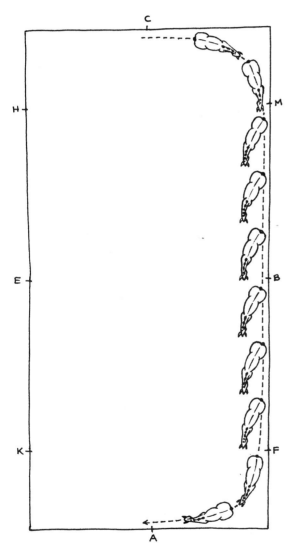

Renvers

(Right) Daniel and Bright Spark showing good positioning and bend in renvers

the outside. You may also find that if you are on the long side and you try to push the quarters out, the horse will resent this quite strongly; whereas if you give him clearance from the side of the school, and thereby room to manoeuvre, you will find him much more confident about doing what you ask.

THE PRINCIPLES OF LATERAL WORK

It is wise to approach all the lateral movements by sending the horse on a little more freely than he would normally be asked. Then allow him to relax back into his normal stride before positioning him ready for the movement that you wish to perform. When horses are learning new movements, particularly the lateral ones, they will very readily lose impulsion during the execution of the movement, which will result in a trot that is less than the ideal in which to perform the lateral work. So by asking the horse to move more energetically forwards, then allowing him to relax as you move into the lateral work, his level of stride is maintained, and he is less likely to fall behind the rider's pushing aids.

The most important thing in all of these movements is that the horse does not fall behind the rider's leg. A common and easy mistake to make in lateral work is that the rider starts to drive the horse forwards by using the outside leg, whose main use should be in pushing the quarters either in or out. This will be in opposition to the desired effect, and will nearly always lead to the horse stopping, or becoming more restrained in his stride. It is therefore of great importance that you maintain the use of both your legs in lateral work, so if the horse should fall behind the desired way of going you can quite easily push him on, allow with the hand and straighten him up to establish the forward movement once again, before re-establishing the lateral movement. This may take once or twice around the school, or maybe only a couple of steps.

Do not become so involved with getting the horse to perform lateral work as to neglect his basic way of going, because this is the only way of preventing these movements from degenerating into tricks. Keep in mind that lateral work is but a part of the classical training of the horse, and should always be underpinned by the basic work the horse would be expected to do on straight lines and circles.

As with all these movements, once they are established, practise them by moving from a straight line into the movement, or from one movement into another. This will provide an opportunity to reiterate the basic way of going to the horse, and to correct any problems that may occur. Work such as this will also aid the horse's physical development and boost his mental confidence once he realises that he *can* actually do as you ask him. One of the greatest dangers of teaching the horse anything new is that his own tension will make him stiff and rigid; as a rider you do actually have to try and overcome this as quickly as possible. This sort of work may also help with horses that have been spoilt in their training, or with slightly older horses to supple them up. The more that lateral work is practised, the more independent the horse will become of the rein, needing it less for support, and the more he will listen to your bodyweight as an aid asking him to do whatever you require of him.

TEACHING HALF-PASS

Having established the travers, the half-pass can then be introduced. The time-span required to develop the half-pass from travers may be only a few minutes for very talented horses, or several weeks for those with slightly less capability, or for those which really resist and resent the idea of moving sideways. There are horses which do very positively resent being asked to cross their legs over in a certain direction, and these need to be handled with a little bit of tact otherwise they could become quite resistant, even to the point of starting to nap.

I find the easiest way to introduce the half-pass is quite simply to take the horse across the diagonal, at first on a straight line. Alternatively, make a half turn at the end of the long side which brings you up the centre line, and travel across the diagonal in a straight line to the opposite corner from which you have just come. As you come

Kirsty Mepham on Dikkiloo in half-pass to the right from the front...and behind

round the corner onto the centre line, point the horse's head specifically at the corner or marker to which you wish to go; if the horse is a little sluggish, these diagonals can be ridden in medium trot, but if he is moving enthusiastically forwards, he can simply be ridden as you would do going large, or on the circle.

Having established these principles several times, you can start teaching him thus: for the last two or three strides of the diagonal – making sure that his head is pointing at the marker towards which you are travelling and that he has enough impulsion – quietly push his quarters to the inside of the line upon which he is travelling. In other words, the horse is asked to perform travers on the diagonal. Approaching the half-pass in such a way will make sure that the horse's desire to go forwards is not forsaken, and the rider's aim in riding towards a specific marker will also be fulfilled.

When this exercise is first practised, you may find that the horse will drift off the line on which you are travelling: in which case it is a very simple matter of closing your legs, easing your hands and riding more forwards until you re-establish your direction of travel, before repeating the exercise. However in my experience most horses, once you have established the line upon which they are to travel before introducing the movement, will be very happy to travel slightly quarters in and still maintain the line. So in this case, as in the case also of the normal travers, the horse will remain travelling along your chosen line.

If the angle of the travers is increased through repeated attempts at performing it, until the point is reached where the quarters are just fractionally behind the shoulder, then a very reasonable half-pass will have been established; and this can be finely tuned by adjusting the pace and positioning

(Left) Daniel and Bright Spark in half-pass left

(Right) The shoulder-in positioning before the horse is taken into half-pass right

of the horse until the true half-pass position is achieved. With practice, the half-passes can be made deeper or shallower by aiming the horse for different points along the arena. Be careful, however, not to ask the horse for a half-pass which is too steep for him to be able to perform at his level of training.

Generally speaking, I find it best when practising the half-pass with a fairly inexperienced horse to move him from the centre line to the side of the arena. The horse tends to move in this direction anyway, and this can then be enhanced and manipulated by the rider to form the half-pass. In addition to this, the horse will have a strong inside bend on the turn onto the centre line, which in itself is good preparation for the half-pass. When

taking the horse from the long side, prepare him for the movement by riding shoulder-in; when the shoulder-in is fully established and the head and neck are pointing at the marker at which you wish to aim, the horse can then be pushed forwards and slightly thinking travers, off the track along the line that you have chosen.

Moving on to slightly more complicated half-passes, these include the 'counter change of hand', more commonly known as the 'zig-zag half-pass'. In this, the horse moves from one half-pass direction into the opposite one, by changing his flexion and bend. I find it best to teach this series of half-passes to both rider and horse by breaking them down into constituent parts. A sensible way to begin the movement is by starting either at the end

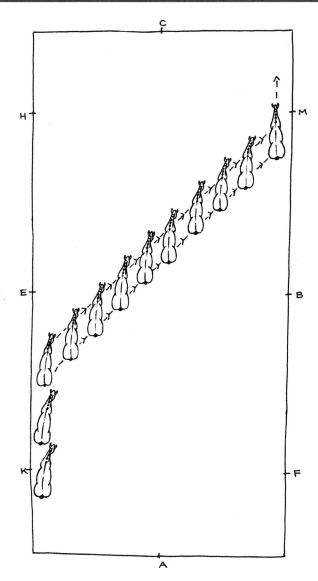

prepare the horse, followed by half-pass, then a few strides of travelling straight, before re-establishing the shoulder-in in the opposite direction, and then finally the new half pass. This sequence can be repeated several times. Never hurry the exercise: if changes of hand are rushed, the best you will achieve is a rather broken and awkward change of direction. If planned well, the movement can look extremely easy, appearing to the onlooker that you are simply flowing from one movement to the next.

Performing the half-pass in canter is a natural progression from the trot half-pass, and in many cases it is easier for the horse than performing the movement in trot. This is due to the horse's natural three-beat rhythm in canter and because the horse is pushing from one hind leg to the opposing foreleg. In the canter, it is important not to allow the horse to run sideways by keeping him firmly positioned between both your legs and hands, so that he is being ridden at all times from his tail, over his back to his poll, rather than from one side of his body to the other. In this way the horse will maintain both his direction and forward movement.

As with the trot, it is to introduce the canter half-pass initially by taking the horse down the centre line and diagonally onto the track in half-pass, then continuing straight down the long side, going round the corners in counter-canter until the horse re-establishes his balance. Continuing in counter-canter will also ensure that the horse has maintained his balance in the half-pass. Once established, change the rein and canter lead and practise the movement on the other rein. Once the horse understands what is required of him in the half-pass movement in all the paces, he can then be corrected and the exercises repeated. A very useful way to do this, particularly in the canter, is to half-pass from the beginning of the long side to the centre line and then to proceed straight ahead down the centre line, maintaining the lead of the canter. At the end of the centre line, make a turn to the direction in which the horse is cantering before immediately performing the whole movement again from the beginning of the next long side. Half-passing from the centre line to the long side, however, will involve changing the rein and will thereby allow only intermittent practice of the half-pass on each rein. Any problems can be corrected much more quickly if you stay on one rein and correct the faults, before changing to the other.

of a long side or the centre line, in shoulder-in position. Once established in the shoulder-in position, the horse can be ridden forwards into the half-pass. Having established this half-pass, allow him to straighten for a few strides, and then change the bend and direction by establishing firstly the shoulder-in position in the other direction.

The shoulder-in position should be maintained for as long as it takes to settle the horse, thus making sure that he is fully prepared to execute a good half-pass in that direction. As the whole movement is tidied up and becomes more polished, only a few strides of straightness and shoulder-in are performed before each half-pass, until the change-over takes only a couple of seconds. In short then, the movement involves shoulder-in to

PROBLEMS WITH MEDIUM AND EXTENDED PACES

What if my horse rushes off or breaks into canter when I ask him to extend?

To deal with this problem you have to go back to the basic preparation of the movement, rather than attempt to remedy the movement itself. The key to getting a good extension is to prepare the horse well on the short side, or that part of the arena you are riding on before you go into the extension. With a horse that rushes off it is usually this preparation that has not been thorough enough. Also, the chances are that the rider has asked the horse to go into extension too rapidly upon coming onto the diagonal or the long side. When this happens, back off slightly and take a little longer to get into the extension so that the transition is more progressive. The horse will then have a few more strides to reach his peak lengthening of stride, or the degree of lengthening that you require from him.

A good way to do this is to ask for the extension to start half-way along the short side, so that you are increasing the horse's stride step by step; as you turn the corner, gradually allow him to go longer and longer so that as you reach the long side, you should have a half-decent extension. It may mean initially that he is only giving you the amount of extension you require for the last half to third of the diagonal or long side you are on, but this does not matter if you are consistent in the approach that you use, as the horse will gradually give you the extension you require over a shorter number

of strides and so he will more quickly get into full extension.

If a horse breaks into canter across the diagonal as I ask him to go into medium trot, I do one of two things: initially I will drive him on in canter and will not haul him back into trot, even though this may be my first reaction. I will do this three or four times, and often I find that the horse will run away; but once he realises that he is required to work just as hard in the canter, he will often give up the idea of changing the pace to resist me. Combined with a slightly more subtle approach to the lengthening, I find that this exercise is often quite successful in getting the horse to stretch his stride without breaking.

However, if a horse still consistently breaks after five or six attempts I will bring him back quite firmly, and sometimes quite sharply, out of the canter to a walk. Then, after patting him on the neck, I will ask him to go forwards into the trot and to repeat the beginning of the lengthening phase until he reaches the lengthening I require. I would not use this method until I had repeatedly tried the 'pushing on' method first, as I find this the more successful of the two. Sometimes a horse will repeatedly and disobediently break into canter if he thinks it is an easy way out. In this instance I will quite sharply check him back out of the movement, usually into walk, and then repeat the whole procedure again. This sometimes means that I have to go several times around the school, or describe a figure of eight repeatedly, until I start getting a few lengthened strides without the tendency to break.

As soon as you achieve these

few lengthened strides – even if they are not as many as you would like – as long as they are in the right direction, I would then pat the horse and make a fuss of him, before repeating the exercise again. It is extremely important to mix reprimand with reward.

What if my horse merely quickens his pace, or starts to run when I ask him to extend?

There are several ways of checking whether you are achieving lengthening or whether you are just getting a quickening of the pace. One of the simplest ways is to pick two fixed points on the arena, either on the long side of the whole diagonal measuring a distance of 10–20 metres, and count the number of strides that your horse takes in its ordinary trot to cover this distance. For instance, if it takes you ten strides to cover the set distance, next time try and cover the distance in less – say, six or eight strides. By doing this you will very soon know if your horse is only quickening or if he is actually stretching his stride; if he is truly taking longer steps he will need fewer to cover the distance.

One of the problems which often occurs in the extended trot with the more inexperienced rider is that the horse runs: this means that he does not increase the length of his stride in the moment of suspension, but scuttles along faster, with more, quick strides per minute rather than fewer, longer strides per minute. Ideally in the extended trot the rhythm should remain more or less the same; in reality it will vary slightly according to the horse's ability to lengthen. It is important to keep a check upon yourself as to whether the horse is truly lengthening or merely quickening, and this should be done for all paces, from walk to canter. If the horse is truly lengthening his stride, he will take fewer strides to cover the distance between the designated markers. If, on the other hand, you count the same number of strides in your attempted extended trot and extended canter as you counted in collected trot and collected canter, then there is no way that the horse can be achieving any extension – it can only be quickening.

By concentrating like this you will find it easy, even with the most difficult horses, to get their stride gradually to stretch. Obviously, how good their stride becomes depends on the horse's own natural ability to lengthen or shorten his stride. Taking that into account, it is still a very good way of assessing whether lengthening has been achieved or whether the rider has only been able to quicken the horse's stride.

PROBLEMS WITH LATERAL WORK

What if my horse's quarters fall in or out?

As with all the other lateral work, problems such as this can easily be corrected by first riding forwards. Straighten the horse up and send him on by closing your legs and slightly allowing with your hands in order to push him into a much more active trot in which you can gain

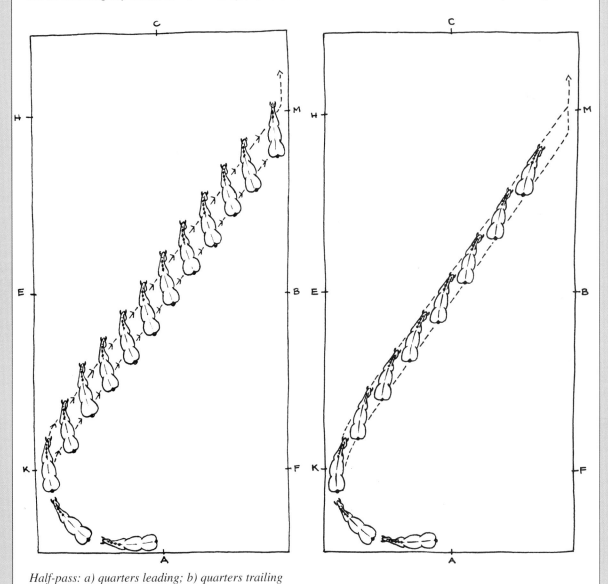

Half-pass: a) quarters leading; b) quarters trailing

greater control of the quarters. If you try to control the quarters without establishing the forward movement you will end up simply chasing the horse around the arena, either over- or under-correcting the position of the quarters. If the horse is moving forwards, the quarters can be controlled with relative ease.

What if my horse really resists being asked to move sideways in the half-pass?

There are several ways of dealing with this problem. One of the methods I will use if the horse really has difficulties maintaining his bend in the half-pass is to revert to doing shoulder-in and travers until he begins to listen to his rider. If on the other hand his problem really is to do with going sideways, from one side of the arena to the other, and if it can't be overcome by going back to riding shoulder-in, renvers and travers, then try the following: keep the horse really straight once turned down the centre line, and if anything, take his head in the wrong direction so you can push him sideways more readily. So for example on the left rein, take the horse down the centre line, but feel the right rein and so take his head slightly the wrong way. Making sure that he is going actively forwards again, ask him with your outside (right) leg to start to drift towards the long side. If this is practised several times, the horse should begin to respond, moving away and over from your right leg. Then you can start to reintroduce the travers approach to the half-pass, so that the correct bend is achieved. Most horses, if worked logically through this problem, will find the solution and come to perform the movement with relative ease.

What if my horse resents being asked to move sideways because he is afraid of banging his legs together?

This fear usually derives from the point in the movement where the horse is liable either to brush into, or tread on his opposite leg, and obviously he will not be willing to move in such a way as to risk this situation because it would cause him a great deal of discomfort. If he does unfortunately brush once or twice, he may well then resent being asked to do the movement again.

When a problem such as this arises, it is the rider's responsibility to make sure that the next time he asks the horse to repeat the movement, he decreases the angle at which it is performed so that the hind legs or the forelegs only barely cross over. Continue in this way for several metres before straightening the horse up again and pushing him forwards; then he can be asked to perform the movement once again, and again so that his legs hardly

cross over. By repeating this exercise several times, the horse will hopefully gain confidence as he learns that performing the movement does not cause him any discomfort; he can then once again be asked for a greater degree of angle, which he should accomplish without showing any resistance.

Remember that a resistance is often a defence: the horse will often just be defending himself against what he sees as an assault from the rider who is asking him to do something which he thinks will hurt him, or that he feels he can't do. It is therefore very much down to the rider to ask him to perform little and often, rather than all at once, until his confidence builds up to the point where he feels quite happy to offer any of the lateral work.

You can see by looking at the jaw crossing and the muscles of the neck that this horse is blocking and stiffening against the rein

What if my horse stiffens up and resists me after doing only a few strides of lateral work?

I have often seen horses blocking against their riders after only a few strides of lateral work – for example, the half-pass – and when pushed by the rider to continue, they often become quite nappy, rearing up and running away from the rider's leg. It is therefore very important, especially with the more nervy horse, to reassure him as you are executing the movement. Also, whilst riding him sideways, make sure that the horse always has a 'forward' escape route so that any time he begins to resist, you simply have to close your legs, ease the reins, and send him forwards in a straight line out of the half-pass.

When this can be achieved, you will have the answer to many of the horse's problems with lateral work, as one of the main reasons for it failing, is because the horse is not moving sufficiently forwards – instead of taking a steady, even, forward stride, he may be compromising by taking a slightly larger sideways stride than he is taking a forward one. If this happens, once again, the chances of the horse banging his legs together will be increased, and as a result his confidence in the rider will decrease.

So, once again, perform lateral work little and often, with repeated small strides, building up gradually to a greater number of strides until the horse is completely confident

(Left) The horse is beginning to stiffen against the rein

(Right) The horse is now stiffening against the rein and refusing to move off the leg. If this problem is left unchecked it is easy to see how something more serious, such as a rear, could occur

about doing what he is asked to do. This is far better than bullying him into doing it, so that he performs only under duress; in which case you will never have the lightness and harmony that you will achieve when the horse has been taught the movements with sympathy and understanding, and will perform them for the rider happily and with ease.

6

THE FLYING CHANGE

The flying change occurs when the horse performs a change of lead in the air. This occurs during the period just before and during the moment of suspension of the canter stride, when the pair of legs on one side of the horse's body are 'overtaken' by the lateral pair of legs on the opposite side. Therefore a horse cantering on the right lead – whose sequence of legs after a moment of suspension is the left hind first to the floor, then the diagonal pair of right hind and left fore, followed by the right fore – would begin to 'change' as he pushes up into the following moment of suspension with his right hind so that the left hind and left fore move together through the air. At this moment the right fore begins to move in sequence with the left hind as the left fore extends to become the new leading leg. This sequence is obviously converse for the change from left to right.

As if this isn't enough to confuse all concerned, the flying changes may be performed not only singly, but also sequentially, that is repeatedly after a certain number of strides: for example, every 4, 3, and 2 strides and at every stride.

Whilst he may not be as collected during the change as in his normal canter, the horse should maintain his way of going and remain in lively self-carriage.

Flying changes are introduced to the horse once he is sufficiently established at medium level to have confidence in the rider's aids and therefore not likely to be intimidated by this sort of work. Whilst the flying change is usually introduced at this stage in the horse's training, there are some horses that show a very easy and clear aptitude to performing these changes when they are a lot younger. In this case they usually have such good natural balance that to do a flying change with an experienced rider will actually not really intimidate them at all, but will possibly serve to improve their natural way of going by making their canter bolder and their backs softer. These horses are, however, best considered the exception rather than the rule, and should only really be dealt with at an earlier stage by the more experienced rider.

As a general rule the flying change is therefore introduced in the more advanced training stages of a horse. In preparation for the changes, he should be able to perform with ease counter-canter as well as true canter and also simple changes of lead in the canter through both walk and trot. There are several ways of beginning to teach the horse the flying change. The most common way is to establish the horse in counter-canter and when he is collected, to ask him for a change of lead from counter-canter into true canter.

The best way of approaching the preparation for the flying change – which is, after all, what the success or failure of the change will depend on – is to teach the horse to collect up and to move forwards very easily in the canter itself, so that he can almost perform a couple of strides not quite on the spot, but very nearly, and then spring forwards easily into a medium canter, whilst also as easily being able to collect at the other end. By doing simple changes, the horse can be made alert and attentive to the rider's aids and once this is achieved, the flying change can be introduced properly.

I firmly believe that the positioning of the weight of the rider in the correct way helps to get most changes correct if not the first time, then certainly within the first few attempts. This involves a study of the way in which the horse actually canters. If one imagines a horse cantering on the right lead, after a clear moment of suspension, the first leg to touch the ground will be the left hind leg. He will then strike the ground, if the canter is correct, with the right hind leg and the left foreleg simultaneously, followed by the right foreleg. Conversely in a left canter after the moment of suspension, the horse will strike the ground with the right hind leg, followed by the left hind leg and the right foreleg simultaneously and then the left foreleg. In effect, the horse is actually cantering from one corner of his body through to the opposite corner.

In the flying change you are asking the horse in the moment of suspension of the canter actually to swap this whole sequence of footfalls. Some people explain this as the horse changing the lead in the air and landing with the opposite hind leg together; in other words actually suggesting that he has changed his diagonal. This is an approach which is worth thinking about, although I view the situation slightly differently, in that if the horse is cantering, he creates a sequence of footfalls which is preceded by a moment of suspension and followed by a moment of suspension.

As the horse is on the way up into the air after a particular sequence of footfalls, depending upon which canter lead he is on (in this case, we will assume the right canter lead is established), his inside pair of legs, that is to say the left hind and left front leg, actually move forwards and overtake the right hind and front legs, placing the horse onto the new left lead. Seen from this point of view, the flying change can be regarded as more of a lateral movement than a simple change of diagonal.

Looking at the horse's actions in a little more detail may help the rider to understand more clearly what he is asking of the horse, and he will therefore be able to refine his aids accordingly. So, in appraisal, if the horse is cantering to the right, he will have a moment of suspension, followed by the placing of the left hind leg on the ground, then the right hind leg and the left foreleg together, then the right foreleg. When the right foreleg has touched the ground, the horse will then be on his way up into the moment of suspension again. As he goes up into this moment, to perform a flying change his left hind leg and left foreleg must overtake the right hind leg and right foreleg so that he therefore lands with the right hind leg first on the ground, followed by the diagonal pair of the right foreleg and the left hind leg, and then the left foreleg. If the horse manages this, he will have completed a flying change quite successfully.

The next important issue is how the rider goes about effecting this swapping of legs. The first thing is to get the horse bouncing actively and attentively along in the canter in such a way that he

is really using himself. The canter should, however, be slightly more contained, otherwise the horse may feel that he is too free, and that he will therefore risk hurting himself by striking his legs together, and this will cause him to fail to fly the change. If this happens, the horse's confidence will have been knocked and he will in the future be wary of trusting the rider. In the same way, if he lands in an untidy heap after the change, or if he lands uncomfortably, it will also make him more wary of taking off initially to perform the change.

A bouncy but contained canter should therefore be achieved and at the same time, the counter-canter established. Assuming the horse is still on the right lead, he will be thrusting from his left hind leg up and over through the diagonal pair of the right hind leg and left foreleg into the right foreleg. Just prior to the change, collect the horse and ask him to jump a little more forwards and a little higher so that some of his forward push is translated into upward lift.

The rider has to be very aware of how he is sitting on the approach to the change: assuming he is sitting correctly with the horse, he will be sitting a little from the left seatbone, pushing through into the right foreleg, to keep the canter going. However, what he has to do is to even his weight out so that on the approach to the change he is sitting more evenly. At the same time, he must use both his legs to maintain the degree of jump and lift of the canter. The horse must then be asked carefully to change the lead to the inside. To help him to do this, the rider can sit a little onto the right seatbone, in effect trapping the right hind leg and delaying it fractionally, to allow the left hind leg and foreleg to overtake. The right foreleg doesn't need to be worried about too much as it tends to follow the sequence of footfalls quite naturally.

Imagine riding the horse up into the change: just at the moment you take off into the air to perform the change, sit not too heavily, but positively above the right hind leg and perform a slight half-halt with your seat, leg and right rein at the same time as moving your leg into the new canter position; that is to say, your inside leg moves forwards against the girth and your right leg moves back and indicates the change of canter lead. If the right rein holds off just slightly and the inside rein allows a little bit of freedom at just the right time, the horse will then push off into the moment of suspension a

Flying change to the left
(Left) Bright Spark in the stride preceeding the flying change stride

(Centre) The moment of suspension during which he changes his lead
(Right) The completion of the flying change to the left

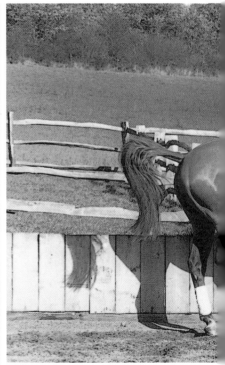

Flying change to the right
(Left) The horse just leaving the ground and beginning to change the lead

(Centre) The new lead beginning to establish
(Right) The completion of the flying change to the right

little more off the right hind leg. Simultaneously he should allow the inside hind leg and inside foreleg to come through and past the outside legs.

The rider must sit very still and straight whilst the horse is changing his legs, but he must also be very careful not to sit in a position that may cause the horse to land awkwardly after the flying change. Should he land in a jarring fashion upon the horse's back, the horse will lose confidence and will be unlikely to perform the change with willingness and ease at his next attempt. At this stage it is therefore very much a matter of the rider positioning himself most conveniently to allow the horse he is riding to perform this swapping of legs without causing it any degree of discomfort.

The flying change can be performed at several points around the arena. For example, the horse can be counter-cantered down the long side, then taken onto a large counter-canter circle and asked to change as he crosses the centre line. Another way in which to approach the flying change is to canter on the true lead up the long side, and perform a half 8 to 10-metre circle allowing the horse to return to the track, at which point the change is asked for. Alternatively, the horse can be made to go from canter to walk and back to canter, perform the flying change, canter a couple of strides and then return back into walk. This last approach can be a very useful way of settling down horses which try to rush off after changing.

Some people prefer to perform the flying change from the half-pass position, in that they push the horse firmly in the direction of the particular half-pass and then as they approach the track, they ask the horse to go a little in the other direction, asking him at this point to perform a flying change. All of these methods have their benefits, but the individual horse must be taken into consideration and an approach employed that will suit that particular horse's way of going. Above all, the method chosen should serve to increase the horse's confidence, making him feel comfortable about performing the change.

What makes a flying change correct and classical is when it is performed with a good springing and swinging canter, with the horse maintaining his desire to go forwards, his rhythm,

Flying change to the right. The weight change of the rider is very noticeable here

his outline and degree of self-carriage, whilst also remaining on a straight line as he performs the change. The change should be full of expression, with the horse appearing to execute it willingly and at ease, and not merely as a subservient swapping of legs. The hindquarters should be engaged throughout the approach to the change, and in the change itself. Once executed, the horse should proceed as if nothing has disturbed his balance at all.

These are all ideal situations. With many horses, the methods and requirements I have described will be conditioned in order to get the horse to do a flying change. When the horse is doing a change he will almost certainly lose his balance at some stage or another in the procedure. The rider must therefore be prepared to counter this loss of balance.

MULTIPLE OR 'TEMPI' CHANGES

Once the horse is thoroughly established at individual flying changes and is able to perform them at any point around the arena from a multitude of different angles and directions without getting anxious by what is being asked of him, and once he can actually express the change clearly, then it is time that the trainer considered teaching the horse the multiple or 'tempi' changes: that is, flying changes with a certain number of strides between each of them. For competition purposes, the tempi changes are usually performed either every fourth, third, second or every stride.

The way that I prepare the horse for the tempi changes is to ask him to change frequently when going across any diagonal or down any long side. Initially, don't worry about counting the number of strides between the changes; for example a change can be made at the beginning of the long side, one in the middle and another at the end, and in this way the horse has a chance to recover his balance sufficiently before executing the next change.

Once this pattern of changes has been established and the horse is quite confident, I will progress to riding serpentine loops where on each change of direction I can ask the horse to execute a flying change. To start with I will only ride about three or four loops (in a 60 x 20 metre arena), but later I progress to riding as many loops as can be fitted in by almost doubling back on myself at the end of each loop. I will continue to the next loop whether or not each change is successful, and here lies the advantage in riding many loops, in that if the horse does ride the change incorrectly, there are many more opportunities to correct it.

When the horse is happy with performing the changes on the serpentine, and also happy with performing more regular flying changes around the outside of the school and possibly across the diagonal, then you can start insisting that he perform the changes with a set number of canter strides in between each one. To start with, ride about eight to ten canter strides between each change until the horse is confident, and then reduce this number systematically until there are only four, three or two canter strides between the changes. It is important that each change remains obedient to the rider's aids, and also remains straight on the diagonal or long side so that the horse doesn't lose his positioning, but moves happily forwards along it; this ensures that he can be asked to perform another flying change whenever required.

Technically tempi changes are only classified as such when either four or a lesser number of canter strides are performed between each change. In the four-tempi changes, the horse should execute a flying change, take three normal canter strides, then on the fourth canter stride perform a change to the new direction, after which he will perform another three normal canter strides and on the fourth, change once again to the opposite direction. When you count the number of strides between each change it is not really a good idea to count 'one, two, three, four,' because on the count of 'four' you should actually be performing the change. A better technique is for the rider to count 'one, two, three change'. Although a seemingly trivial point, I have found that it has helped many riders to establish correctly the required number of strides between each change.

It is not unusual to find that horses will often cope more easily when asked to do three-time changes rather than four-time changes. This is mainly because the horse has less time in which to lose his concentration and balance when having to ride only three strides between each change instead of four, and although this may seem rather a ridiculous assumption in most cases it is correct.

Once the four- and three-tempi changes are established, it is then fairly easy and only a matter of time to progress to teaching the horse the two-tempi changes. Whilst the four- and three-tempi changes can be attempted by asking for three or maybe even four consecutive changes, I often find it wise when starting the two-tempi changes just to ask for two and then to have a break, before asking for another two and so on. This is because the horse needs to develop a greater degree of balance to keep himself engaged, straight and in self-carriage through the changes.

With the two-tempi changes, you are in effect asking the horse to change, take a normal stride and then to change again. This means that there is actually very little time to correct any loss of balance, especially with the less experienced horse. The horse should therefore get used to executing a change a stride, and also a change at various points around the arena. It should then take only a short time – a couple of days to a week – before several two-time changes in a row can be performed.

The correct execution of the tempi changes really comes down to the rider's ability to count them correctly, and this can only be dealt with through practice on the part of the rider. It is quite interesting that if you sit down and think too hard about counting the number of strides in between each change, it is easy for you to become more confused than if you were on the horse, preferably under the instruction of a decent trainer, and actually feeling the rights and wrongs of what both you and your horse are doing as you go along. Even better is for the rider to have had the opportunity to ride a horse that is already established and trained in the movement that he is trying to teach to his own inexperienced horse, so that it is not simply a case of the 'blind leading the blind'. This is particularly true in the case of the tempi changes, where to perform them properly, you really have to be applying the right aid at the right time and be very aware of your body position and the various weight-related aids that you will be using.

The next stage after teaching the horse the four-through to two-tempi changes, is to introduce the one-time changes. In my experience, if you had particular difficulties teaching the horse the single changes, then it is often the case that you will find similar problems repeating themselves in the one-tempi changes. There are, as with all the movements, many ways to teach the horse the one-tempi changes. Some people promote the idea of doing first of all one change, and then two, followed by three, four and so on. There is absolutely nothing wrong with this approach, as long as the rider is of the correct mentality, and aware of what he is trying to achieve.

However, the method I find most useful is initially to reach the horse what I call the 'one-two' or 'flip-flop' changes. By this method, if the horse is cantering on the right leg, I will ask him to change to the left and then immediately back to the right. This would be one complete 'one-two' change. I will then repeat this so that the horse changes from the left to the right and immediately back to the left again. The idea of this exercise is that he becomes proficient and confident in doing a change of stride from either direction; starting from either the left or the right leg. It is extremely important, particularly with the one-time changes, that in this initial learning stage the horse is not asked to do the changes during a turn or on a corner. Therefore make sure that there is always enough room after the turn or corner to enable you to re-establish the horse's balance before attempting further change work. Once the horse is happy in performing these 'one-two' changes, I will then ask him to perform them in various places around the arena – I will ask for two changes maybe at the beginning of the long side, two in the middle and two at the end.

At this stage, the 'one-two' changes can be gradually joined up. The way in which I prefer to do this – which is by no means the only way, but simply the one I find most efficient – is to ride one 'one-two' set of changes, before proceeding for a certain number of strides – perhaps two, four or even six – and then performing the 'one-two' movement again. Gradually the number of strides between each 'one-two' movement can be reduced, and the horse can be asked to perform it with greater frequency, depending of course on his capabilities.

I usually reduce the number of strides between each 'one-two' movement to two strides. So, for example, I may ask the horse to change left and right, and then canter for two strides on the right leg, before asking him to change left and then right again. This exercise must then be repeated on the other rein so that the horse is changing this time from the right to the left.

After the horse has mastered such exercises as these, I will position him somewhere slightly away from the long side of the school – for example, a metre or so in, so that the wall of the school will introduce no conflict – and ask him to perform a 'one-two' and then immediately another 'one-two' again. For this movement the rider must be really alert, precise and quick with his aids. If the horse has been properly prepared, it doesn't usually take very long for him to gain confidence at doing not just two, but four one-time changes; and it certainly doesn't take a lot of imagination to see how he might quite quickly achieve six or eight changes and so on, until you can ask for any number of changes that you wish.

Again it is a personal preference of mine to ask the horse to do an even number of strides. This may simply be due to the way that my mind works, and it may well be that other people find it easier to ask the horse to do one stride, then two, then three, four strides of the changes and so on. I do feel that the method by which you teach your horse the one-tempi changes should be chosen by yourself, and should depend on what you feel most comfortable with. However, if the trainer is to be successful in teaching many different types of horse, he must be able to refer to either method, and indeed to the many other little techniques that one develops as a trainer in order to teach the individual horse that may present certain problems. In other words, if one approach fails, a trainer must always have another which he hopes will lead to success!

Once again, patience and time are key factors here. In the real world, it is quite possible that the rider or trainer gets too carried away, and maybe on one day asks the horse to do far too much. If this situation does occur, and I think most trainers will agree with me that it sometimes does, it is very important to establish what has been learned, and then assess the horse's temperament before pushing on with his training any faster. If the horse lacks, or has even lost confidence, he will be unable to perform bold, free and forward changes and will also be incapable of adding any expression as he does them. It is, after all, of very little use having a horse which executes clockwork changes if all the classical elements which require the horse to become more beautiful in his way of going are damaged to the extent that the horse risks becoming no more than an automaton.

THE FLYING CHANGE

To my mind, the teaching of changes is a really personal aspect of training, because the results can be seen almost immediately and in the same way, the successes and failures become instantly apparent. However, it is important not simply to execute the changes as an end in themselves, but to use them as a test of the horse's carriage and balance. Many horses that struggle in their balance and way of going can undoubtedly be helped by careful and judicious teaching of changes, because in the hands of a good trainer, they can help the horse to gain in confidence and in his expressiveness.

When the horse is confident in performing all the changes right through to one-time changes, there are many things that the rider can do with them, depending on the ability of the horse. For example, a very well-balanced horse will be able to perform even the most difficult of tempi changes on circles and turns. This is often seen in freestyle

A very impressive start to flying change in medium canter for Lahti and Dall'ora Conz (Italy)

tests where the rider wishes to increase the technical difficulty to gain higher marks. For me, however, it is not very nice to see a horse that is wholly capable of doing expressive and confident tempi-changes on a straight line being forced into a situation where he is doing changes on a circle that he can't cope with and which he finds a real struggle. If this is the case, all the harmony and attractiveness of the art of dressage is being sacrificed for nothing more than a trivial exercise to win marks.

It is always wise to remember that the art of training a horse to Advanced or even Grand Prix level is not just to teach him tricks, but to use the movements as a way to test the horse's way of going. This is, after all, all that the movements should really ever be. Anyone can teach tricks, but if the classical way of going is not adhered to while the horse is being taught to do the more difficult and complicated movements, the whole training process will deteriorate into nothing more than a series of trick-training exercises, as I have already tried to emphasise.

• *There are obviously many problems that can be encountered when teaching flying changes, and it is not always correct to say that one is more common than another* •

What if my horse is late behind in the change?

One of the greatest errors that is often made when teaching the horse flying changes is that his confidence is not allowed to develop sufficiently, causing him to make mistakes in executing the changes; more often than not, this involves him being either late behind or early in front. By this we mean that instead of his legs jumping through together and in harmony, either the foreleg or hind leg will be in advance or in arrears in such a way that a double beat is met on the change and the actual new diagonal of the canter is not established.

There are many reasons for this occurring. Some horses tend to be a little more lazy with one leg than the other, whilst most horses are stiffer one way and softer the other and this may be expressed in such a way in the changes. It may also be that the horse is simply just not sufficiently balanced and collected to begin learning the flying changes at all – and rather than be disobedient and do nothing, he may well therefore put in his best offer, the result being that he executes these late or anticipatory changes.

The first thing to establish in such a situation is whether the horse is truly late with one hind leg, or if he is actually being a little anticipatory with a foreleg and is in fact changing through more quickly in front. An experienced rider or trainer will know instinctively the horse that, intending to switch as he puts his aid on, quickly pops the foreleg through in anticipation of the rider's aids, but is then actually in time with the hind leg, and he can do something to correct or prevent the horse from doing this. Equally, most trainers should be able to see very quickly when the horse has been a little late with a hind leg. It is of vital importance to work out which problem is actually occurring as you do the changes, because the solutions to the two different problems are often quite different.

With the horse that is late behind – and this is probably the more common of the two problems – it is very important to improve his degree of engagement, collection and his responsiveness, before he is actually asked to perform the movement. If a horse is a little bit lazy or slow off the leg – in other words, in reacting to the rider – he is quite likely either to ignore the leg aid completely, in which case he won't change at all, or to accept it only grudgingly, in which case he will change in front and then a stride later, or maybe even more than this, he may get round to changing behind. If he is particularly set in his ways, he may even tend to change in front only and remain disunited.

Either way, the remedial work here involves the rider going 'back to basics' to a certain extent – though by this I don't mean for weeks, but often just for a few moments to allow the horse to become attentive and active enough and to make sure that he has enough time to register what is being asked of him. It will help to take the horse back through the simple changes of leg – canter, walk and then canter again – on both leads. It may also help to put the whip in the outside hand. For example if the horse is being asked to change from left to right, the whip will be put in the left hand, and for a couple of preceding strides and at the moment of asking the horse to change, he should be given a few light flicks with it, to reinforce the seat and leg aids of the rider and to ensure that he jumps through cleanly in the change.

It will also help greatly if the horse is sent forwards so that he moves from collected to medium or extended canter and then back again to the collected pace. This will ensure that the bounce and height of his canter stride is improved to the extent that he gains more lift and therefore gets more time in the air; this will in turn allow him more time to draw the hind legs through and ensure that the change is clean.

If a horse repeatedly lands awkwardly or uncomfortably, this could also be a reason why he would be a little cautious about drawing his legs through, because he may feel that he will lose his balance, or possibly strike into himself. This for him is how it is for us when we trip over our own feet or stumble awkwardly: if he effectively stubs his toes, or jars his frame whilst being asked to do a change, he will naturally be cautious to give the change when he is asked again. It therefore is a matter of going back and making the horse alert and responsive to the aids without him panicking or worrying, so that when he is asked again, he tends to be a little sharper and better able to push the aid through successfully.

With the lazier horse, you may have to cause him to be a little over-active in order for him to push through and execute a clean change. This may slightly unsettle him, but as long as he is rewarded when he has been successful, and if you then repeat the movement with

A clear and expressive flying change at the end of the diagonal. The rider is sitting a little too far to one side

a bit of care and feeling for his way of going, you will not find too many problems with eventually getting him through. It may take a couple of weeks or a month to establish a difficult horse in a change, whereas a horse with better balance and a steadier temperament can often establish the change in a matter of a day. It is totally dependent on the horse's physique and his attitude towards the rider; if he does panic and rush off, the rider should quietly

settle him down before repeating the change again. However, I would actually see the act of a lazy horse getting brighter and sharper in his action and attitude towards the change as a positive step forwards, as long as it isn't over-emphasised. All these techniques should be tempered with a little bit of care and thought to avoid any further unnecessary problems.

The other problem, of changing early in front, is usually one that is

associated with the more fraught and uptight horse – although it is by no means an exclusive problem, and may equally occur with the more laid-back horse. However, more often than not it is the sharp horse that is trying to please the rider and getting slightly over-enthusiastic, so that as the rider slightly alters his position to ask for the change, he will jump through in front in anticipation of the rider's aid. He will then usually complete the change by jumping through behind in a stride or so, as the rider actually applies the aids for the change. It is for this reason that it is so important to decipher between the change that is early in front and that which is late behind.

The corrections for this particular problem will depend on the temperament of the horse, whether or not he is coming through quickly in front for the change because he is a little worried, or is coming through late behind because he has a more laid-back tendency and is possibly prone to being a little lazy. In the case of the horse that gets worried, it is wise for the rider to close his legs more firmly around the horse to hold him firmly through the change, and so prevent him from jumping through early in front. For example, in asking the horse to change to the right from a left canter lead, firmly close your upper leg, whilst also keeping your lower leg around the horse's side to hold him on his left canter lead. Give him plenty of warning that you are about to ask for a change, but for several attempts do not actually execute the change so the horse learns that he must not anticipate the aids. In effect, you are simply collecting the horse up to the point where he will

be only a stride or so away from the change, and then relaxing him again by not actually asking for the movement to be completed. When the horse has learned to accept the aid, then it becomes easier to make him wait longer for the leg aid before he changes. In the case of such anticipatory horses, it is important to keep a steady, somewhat firm hold on the reins so that they are held positively between leg and hand. It helps to keep an even feel on both reins and to quite emphatically push the change through, but without applying twisting or swinging leg aids. If, however, the horse gains more confidence by being pushed slightly sideways in the change, for me this is then acceptable, so long as the rider realises that he will eventually have to ride the changes straight.

In the ideal situation, the horse will change straight through, although in the real world this is often not the case; what one must never compromise is the fact that eventually the horse must learn how to do the change in the correct way. And with the horse that anticipates the leg aid it is also important that the aid is neither too large in its movement nor too forceful in its action, although none of its positive effect should be compromised. The horse must learn to recognise the moment when to do the change, but on the other hand, he must not be intimidated to the point where he gets himself into a real panic; if this situation arises, it will probably take some time for him to settle down, and for his confidence in the aids of the rider to be re-established.

All these problems are more easily corrected by the more experienced rider, who will have felt

them many times before and who will probably have had the benefit of receiving tuition from a good trainer. Naturally, it is much harder for riders working alone to recognise and correct such problems as these, because they are having to work out the solutions for themselves. Again, I emphasise the benefits of establishing the feel of such problems on a schoolmaster, but for those people struggling on their own I would like to remind them that some horses learn very quickly, whilst others need to have the alphabet spelt out to them, as it were, so that they can understand clearly and concisely what is required of them.

Amongst the questions you should ask yourself if you are getting frustrated by the problems that you are encountering are 'Am I being fair to the horse?' and 'Does he really understand what I am asking of him?' It is all too easy to assume that the horse understands exactly what we are asking of him. It is also up to the rider to make sure that he has the trust, faith and confidence of his horse before progressing any further along his chosen course of action.

What if my horse ignores my aids when I ask him for a flying change?
This is a common problem with a clever horse, and certainly with a more laid-back one. It is more than likely that the rider thinks he has set his horse up correctly to do the change, but when he asks the horse to perform the change, it just totally ignores him and carries on cantering.

In some cases a short, sharp kick, or a tap with the stick may be sufficient if the horse has realised the error of his ways and is prepared to toe the line. However, the more crafty horse may actually develop this technique into a regular evasion when asked to do the changes. In this instance it is back to basics again I'm afraid, and the horse must be made to recognise the aids of the rider and to react to them. It is no use whatsoever getting more violent towards the horse, or using a bigger stick; rather, the solution lies simply in causing the horse to activate himself a little more and become more responsive to your aids. I find that just using the legs gently, rather than being tempted into using increasingly heavy leg aids, is often the best way; and if the horse does not respond to your gentle leg application, repeatedly pester him with light taps of the stick until he does respond (the taps should not get increasingly hard, but should remain light each time you use the stick).

If the rider is persistent enough in his application of the aids, whether he is using a stick or not, the horse should start to respond, although it may at first be slightly resentful. So, rather than using a really heavy whip or spur aid, I would prefer to use a gentle leg aid that is then reinforced *repeatedly* by a tap with the whip until a reaction is created. To start with, this reaction may not be quite the one you want, but nevertheless, it shows that the horse is listening to you and is aware of your aids. And once the horse has been taught in this way to be responsive when an aid is applied, then you can start to ask him to perform the movements in the way that you wish him to do.

If you do use a heavier aid in

your attempt to do a flying change, you may well be partly successful in that you may make the horse do the change, but what you will have failed to do is to teach him how to do the change in the way that you would wish him to do it. It is no use saying 'never' with horses. Sometimes it may be necessary to somewhat push the change through just to get your message across to the horse, but this is a method that is best avoided. Really then, all it comes down to is going back to the basic routines so that the horse is alert, attentive and ready to spring through on the change aid when he is asked.

It is quite interesting that when some of the horses displaying this problem of ignoring your change aid are alerted, they will then sometimes become over-responsive and start to rush off. Again, this shouldn't be immediately punished or reprimanded. You have asked the horse to respond more promptly, so you should never clamp down on him if he gives you a little bit more than you ask. If he repeatedly becomes too sharp, then settle him down so as to make him a little less responsive. Thus, what we are really talking about here is a matter of action and reaction: you expect the horse to react to you, and if he doesn't, you ask him to become sharper; if he over-reacts, you then ask him to settle down and become less sharp.

You must always be searching for an equilibrium when dealing with horses. There are no set rules, whilst the guidelines are very firm

An extreme example of a horse severely resisting the rider's aids

and clearly laid down. Usually the determining factor as to which approach is taken is the rider's sensitivity and feeling, and his experience of the problems encountered when training horses. Remember, you are not trying to make the horse do what you want, but to make him want to do what you want.

What if my horse swings sideways in the change?

This problem may involve the horse either swinging his quarters in, or throwing his shoulder out. Obviously, if the changes are to be correct and expressive they must be extremely straight, and performed from a bounding canter with plenty of height to allow the horse to express himself clearly through the change. On some occasions, what can happen is that the horse does his best actually to swap canter leads because the rider has insisted on it, but to achieve it he throws himself about, sometimes quite violently.

If this occurs, it is very important for the rider to regress a few steps before performing the change, and to get the horse first of all confident and comfortable just cantering on a straight line, be it on a diagonal or on a long side, so that he accepts the aids of the rider with ease. Again, this problem can be solved easily by making the horse more alert to the aids, rather than by simply using greater strength to force the horse to do what you have asked of him. Rather, it is a matter of being pedantic about the basic way of going of the horse and going back repeatedly to the simple work that one was trying to teach him at Novice and Medium level, making

sure that this work is truly established before moving on any further.

Having said this, there are also horses that will canter perfectly straight until they are asked to do the flying change, when they suddenly seem to develop this ability to leap to the side! I suspect that this may be because at some stage in teaching the horse to change, he felt very uncomfortable in one of the three basic phases of the change, either in the *approach,* or the *take-off* during which the swapping of the legs is performed, or in the *landing*.

If the horse is unbalanced in the take-off, he is likely to push himself into a difficult position the moment he is asked to swap his legs. This may cause him concern, and it may even cause him to become unbalanced and uncomfortable to the extent where he may actually risk striking his legs together, or at least is fearful of striking his legs together. Obviously this will make him very apprehensive about remaining straight throughout the change. It is unfortunate that we can't just say to these horses, much as we would like to sometimes, 'Look, if you jump straight and clean your legs won't strike!' No, our only means of communication with the horse in this respect is to feel and guide him through the change with the aids. The same can also be said of a horse that performs the take-off and change quite clearly, but for some reason lands extremely uncomfortably, or whose rider lands uncomfortably on his back at the end of the change. A parallel to this is found in show-jumping, where if the landing is repeatedly an uncomfortable thing for the horse,

he is not going to want to take off in the first place. In both cases it is a matter of getting the horse to a stage in his carriage where he feels comfortable carrying the weight of the rider as well as his own bodyweight, and in such a way that he feels happy to be asked to repeat the change of leads.

This problem is a very old and common one, and can often take some time to correct, although there are, in fact, many approaches you can take to overcome it. You may find that sending the horse on more, so that the canter is much less restricted, will help to produce a clean, straight change due to the sheer momentum of the canter. Alternatively, if the horse is a little too free in his way of going, ask him to take shorter strides before and as you make the change, disregarding for the time being the usual convention that the change stride should be big and expressive. In this case the horse should be allowed to do a neat swapping of the legs in a fashion that requires no bounding efforts on his part, and after the change he should be cantered in the same short-strided fashion.

By approaching difficulties with changes in such a way, I am not trying to compromise the expressiveness of the horse, I am merely trying to regain his confidence. If this approach is successful, I will then gradually have to push the horse on to increase the range of his stride, although this must be done very cautiously with the horse that panics on the change. Both these methods are equally applicable to problems with the changes, but it is the rider's feel which should dictate to him which method is of best use at which time.

What if my horse rushes away when I ask him to do the change?

This is a very common problem with sensitive horses. They fear the imbalance, and possibly the clashing of legs that may be caused by this loss of balance when they are asked to change, and so many horses, when they feel they may be asked to do a change, will panic and rush away. Firstly, it is very important to attempt to prevent this happening, although this is not always so simple. As a parallel I was always told that the simplest way to stop a horse bolting was not to let it happen in the first place. However this, too, is not as easy as it sounds and in both instances, once the problem is with you, you have to try and do something about it. For me, taking into account the temperament of the horse and my assessment of his reasons for rushing away, I find the best method of solving this problem is by bringing the horse back quite firmly to walk; with the slightly more naughty-minded horse, I may even have to bring him back sharply to walk. I will then make him wait for me in walk, before quietly cantering him on and asking him to repeat the change. If the horse repeatedly runs away each time I ask for the change, I will continue bringing him firmly back to walk. There are, of course, evasive horses who when asked to walk will hot up and misbehave; this sort you should walk on a straight line or circle until they settle.

As soon as the horse realises that the rider will always stop him rushing away, and starts to respond more easily, it is terribly important that you relax immediately and

make a big fuss of him; you would hope that he will then realise that you have not just been trying to bully him into submission, but to teach him something, and more importantly, to help him understand what you require. In the real world there are obviously occasions when the rider or trainer has to be a little more forceful than he would like to be, but as long as this is tempered by a real feeling for the horse, rewarding him when he performs correctly, then I find that it won't lead to any greater problems. What must never be done is to reprimand the horse without then relaxing him and letting him know that everything is okay. Repeated reprimands will either create the automaton which we are trying to avoid, or make the sensitive horse more worried and frenzied in his attempts to do what the rider asks of him. Again, a good feeling for your horse is the best 'tempering mechanism' that you can have.

What if my horse constantly breaks the sequence of tempi changes?

This problem may occur if, for example, I ask the horse to do a set of four-tempi changes and he puts maybe one-, two- or three-tempis into the sequence without me asking, or if he rushes away in the middle of the sequence. It is a problem that will inevitably occur when you start practising tempi changes, usually due to anticipation or tension on the part of the horse, or even to over-eagerness.

With problems like these, the answers can be found amongst those which correct the same problems encountered in the single flying changes: simply apply these

solutions to the more frequently required changes in the tempi changes sequence. You must however, remember that things happen much more quickly when riding the tempi changes, and it is so much easier for confusion to develop. Remember to plan carefully in your mind, and then to analyse the problems as you go through them; and don't in any way be afraid of applying the basics to the more advanced work, because in most cases, the problem is actually caused by the fact that the basics have not been soundly enough established.

A horse that messes around in the tempi changes is simply spoiling his way of going; his behaviour is usually due to the fact that he hasn't managed to maintain the level of balance and self-carriage which would enable him to do the work with sufficient ease, and has therefore put his own interpretation upon what the rider is asking of him. In this instance it is far better to go down a few steps and sort out the single flying changes, and then go back to practising the tempi changes, rather than trying to carry on which will probably do neither you nor the horse any good at all. However, some horses do get particularly fraught when they are asked to do more frequent changes; it may even be that they find the four- and three-tempi changes easy, and then throw themselves into a panic when asked to do the two-tempi changes. Against, it is just a matter of taking a step back, then doing a little forward planning, and ensuring careful application of the basic way of going, in order to resolve the problem fully.

7

PIROUETTES, PIAFFE AND PASSAGE

Pirouettes, piaffe and passage are usually discussed together because they are the epitome of collection. They characterise everything that is required and all that we are striving to achieve when we work the Novice horse through to becoming an Advanced and even a Grand Prix horse. The level of engagement, the bending of the hock and the sitting down of the hindquarters, whilst still maintaining the energetic elasticity of the stride, are requirements of each of these movements.

PIROUETTES

The pirouette is a movement in which the horse describes a circle on two tracks, with the forehand moving around the haunches so that the radius of the circle is roughly equal to the length of the horse. The inside hind leg steps forwards and describes a very small circle, and the outside hind leg moves forwards and around it. The regularity of the stride must be maintained, as should the impulsion and the desire to move forwards so that the self-carriage of the horse is improved. The quarters should be lowered with a good flexion of the joints of the hind legs. The pirouette can be performed at the walk, canter and piaffe. In canter the pirouette should be of six to eight strides.

The canter pirouette is a movement in which the horse maintains his expression in the canter, whilst lowering his quarters and transferring a lot more weight onto his hind legs; he should then perform a turn around his hindquarters. Turns of various degree can be performed: a full turn of 360 degrees is made when the horse leaves the pirouette at the

same point at which he entered it, having travelled once around his hindquarters. However, several lesser turns than this can be made. The two most common types of pirouette are the half-pirouette, which involves a 180-degree turn, and the full pirouette, which has already been discussed.

Before you begin a pirouette it is necessary to make sure your horse has attained a high enough standard of collection for him to be able to maintain his canter and balance. It is of very little value to try and perform a pirouette if you don't maintain the classical criteria of having a free, forward, springing canter, with three clearly marked beats in the stride, and the horse showing a true lowering and engagement of his hindquarters. It is also necessary to make sure that the horse is able to describe and perform small turns and circles with ease before beginning pirouettes. A useful exercise to check whether in fact the horse is ready, or not, to begin work on pirouettes, is to ride a small 6-metre volte; if he can keep perfectly in balance on the circle and can maintain all the engagement that he had on the straight, then he could start practising pirouettes.

As with all the other advanced work we have discussed, it is best to start by asking only a few strides of the movement from the horse, before relaxing him and moving him forwards. Also, as preparation for performing pirouettes, make sure that the horse can perform shoulder-in and travers in canter. All these are ways of making the horse pliable and flexible, able to respond to the rider's aids, whilst not losing his balance or his desire to go forwards. Once I feel he is happy performing these prepatory exercises, I then ask for a slightly more prolonged period for him to come onto a circle and alternate travers and shoulder-in positions on the circle. Not only does this develop the ability of the horse to travel in both the shoulder-in and the travers position, but also his ability to move from one position to the other.

Once this exercise poses no problems to either rider or horse, it is a very simple matter of reducing the size of the circle you have been working so the horse becomes very collected, with his quarters well lowered. You can then gradually ask the horse to turn his forehand around his quarters. Don't worry if initially the turn is a little too big, or the horse loses his balance; simply ride forwards out of the pirouette before asking him to try again. The key to a successful pirouette lies in whether or not the horse can successfully maintain his balance and his canter. All the time, push him more and more until he gets nearer and nearer the point where he can maintain his weight on his hindquarters; thus the turn becomes really rather incidental of the preparation, something to be added once the horse is properly listening to you.

Another very useful exercise is to practise cantering nearly on the spot and then moving forwards again, so that the horse is happy with jumping and springing in place, and then being pushed on; however, there should be no feeling of rushing away, nor should any of the quality of the canter be lost – although initially as you approach this movement, the horse will invariably lose some of the quality of the canter. The rider will have to use quite positive driving aids to push the horse up into the bridle, to create a feeling not that he has slowed down, but that he is more activated, so the forward speed can then be reduced but impulsion and vitality will not be compromised. What must not happen when the horse is collected, is that he reduces the amount of energy he uses to maintain his canter; if anything, he should ideally be using more energy.

There are several ways of approaching the turn. Again, I find it quite a simple matter to bring the horse onto a small 6–8 metre circle. When I feel his confidence is ample, I will ask him gently to bring his forehand more and more to the inside, whilst maintaining his desire to go forwards in the canter. The moment before the horse gets to the point where he loses his balance, I will bring him out of the pirouette by simply enlarging the circle, so that he keeps the bound of the canter going.

Daniel and Bright Spark performing canter pirouette to the right

This sequence shows Dane performing pirouette to the right

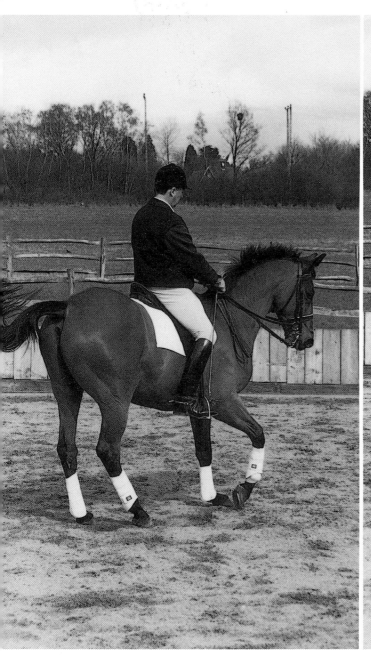

An alternative way to approach the turn of the pirouette is by performing a shoulder-in down the long side in canter. At some stage, usually on approaching the corner, ask the horse to do more or less an about-turn: this will undoubtedly be rather large at this stage, with the horse describing a turn probably around 5 metres in diameter. At the end of the turn, ask the horse to return quietly to the track. It may be useful to ask him to return in half-pass, so that the idea of going forwards and sideways is established in his mind.

It is the rider's responsibility to make sure that he doesn't over-emphasise any of the approaches to the pirouettes that we have discussed. For example if, on approach, the horse's quarters are tucked in too much, because you have attempted to position him in travers, then he will actually take a lot longer to turn his forehand around his quarters. Working out a bit of simple geometry will therefore tell us that whilst the quarters are also moving to the side, the forehand will have to travel a much greater distance to perform a pirouette positioned in such a way. While some horses are definitely helped by performing with quarters in, others need to approach the pirouette from the shoulder-in position. This is actually a very good way of preparing the horse to turn because he already has his shoulders ahead of his quarters, and there will therefore be less of a distance to move the shoulder round the quarters.

An alternative approach is to place the horse on a square based around, for example, X. The aim of this exercise is to canter the straight sides of the square in a slight shoulder-in position, then as the horse comes to the corner of the square, you ask him to perform a small quarter of a pirouette. He can then immediately be asked to go straight again along the next side of the square, before being asked to perform the quarter pirouette again. This exercise is useful because it gives the rider the opportunity to make sure the horse is jumping through, and off his aids, rather than just turning. It is also a good way of making sure that the horse

goes forwards after each section of the turn. When the horse is comfortable doing this work on both reins, it is then an easy matter to tighten the turns a little more. The method of riding a square can also be slightly altered. For example, you can ride down the centre line and perform a half-pirouette at one end, before cantering on down the centre line until you re-establish the balance and carriage in the canter and then performing a half-pirouette at the other end.

The biggest problem the rider will come across when teaching his horse pirouettes is maintaining its desire to move forwards and its balance. Some horses seem to be born with an instinctive ability to perform pirouettes, and find all the advanced, collected work so easy; if you are lucky enough to own or train such a horse, you may not have to take such a long road when teaching pirouettes. For other horses, though, it really is a struggle. With all these horses, whatever their capabilities, it is necessary to make sure that their work is based on the correct lines. The more difficult horse in particular must have his basic, forward way of going constantly re-established so that he becomes more and more comfortable with actually performing the turns, whilst still maintaining his desire to move forwards.

Once the horse has been taught pirouettes, it is then necessary to start placing them strategically, rather than just placing them at random around the school. This simply takes a little practice and planning on the rider's part, and you should think carefully about the geometry of the arena so you can use it to your best advantage. One of the first pirouettes required in competition is usually that of the Prix St Georges test, or a test similar in its requirement. The horse will be asked to go along the diagonal of the school and perform a half-pirouette so that he returns back along that same diagonal; just before he rejoins the track, he will be asked to perform a flying change. Whether I am riding or teaching, I like to approach this movement by imagining clearly in my mind where the diagonal line is. Then if, for example, I am going to do a left pirouette, I will actually place my horse slightly to the right of the diagonal line that I am working on. I will then ask the horse to collect and perform the pirouette so that he turns in such a way that he is still on the right-hand side of the line that he approached on. In other words, he has

Page 122: Jennie Loriston-Clarke and Dutch Gold in pirouette at Goodwood

Page 123: Optimist and Dane in canter pirouette left in Grand Prix competition at Rotterdam

actually pirouetted in a very slightly larger fashion around the diagonal that he was supposed to be on.

Some may view this as cheating, but in my mind, it is simply common sense. To ask a horse, and particularly one that is inexperienced, to pirouette with his hind leg exactly on the spot, is not very sensible. For me, the pirouette should never be totally on the spot unless the horse is so talented that he can raise and lower his inside hind leg, whilst still maintaining his desire to go forwards. Therefore, even with a full canter pirouette, most riders and judges are extremely happy to accept a turn that has a diameter the size of a large serving plate. In this case, the inside hind leg should canter round the circumference of this very small circle, rather than being dead in the middle of it and stamping up and down on the spot. If you actually ask a horse to stick in the middle, it will more than likely lose its impulsion, but far worse, it will probably start to move backwards on the pirouette, for which it will be heavily penalised if under test conditions.

Again the idea is to maintain free, forward movement so that the horse is well prepared along the diagonal, to which he should be slightly off-set. I would suggest here, that the best way to approach the pirouette is by shoulder-in; then when you are nearly at the point at which you desire to do your actual pirouette, really collect the horse, so that he canters, not quite on the spot, but slightly forwards. He should then be asked to turn, which he should do maintaining the same rhythm and balance, without trying either to lose the canter, or to charge forwards. The turn should be made in such a way that the horse is able very quietly to leave the pirouette in the same level of balance and canter that he approached with. It is of very little use performing a half-decent pirouette, and then having the horse stumble all over the place as he tries to recover his balance afterwards. It is therefore useful not only to practise approaching the pirouette in shoulder-in, but also leaving it in shoulder-in.

If, in training, you find that the horse starts to anticipate the pirouette, you really have to ride him forwards along the diagonal line, until he waits for your aid and turns quietly as he is asked. He must neither jump to the side of the leg as you apply the aid for the pirouette, nor must he ignore the inside leg as it pushes and asks him to jump more forwards.

PIAFFE

The piaffe is a highly collected trot on the spot. The quarters should be lowered, with the hind legs carrying the greater part of the horse's weight. The rhythm should be lively but regular and full of impulsion, with the horse showing an obvious desire to move forwards. The poll should be the highest point. The rein contact should be light, and the rider should be as one with the horse.

The piaffe is a movement that requires the horse to 'sit down' and really transfer a lot of his weight and that of the rider onto his hindquarters, whilst still maintaining a really bright and light way of going. He has an awful lot of energy to dispose of at the request of the rider, and in this respect, for me, the piaffe and the extended trot are quite similar, the only difference being that the energy needed for each movement is expressed differently. In both these movements, in order for them to be correct, the horse must be carrying and thrusting with his hind legs so that the forehand becomes lighter and more free.

Some horses have a natural talent for piaffe, and to teach it to them is a very easy task. It can often be just a matter of collecting up the trot, or pushing the horse up from walk into trot and 'capturing the moment'. The majority of horses, however, find it much more difficult and they need to be taught what is required of them. With any horse, it is very important that the process of learning the piaffe is very gradual, particularly so with the horse that does not have a wonderful talent for the movement. With such a horse, it can take a great deal of work from the rider to develop the horse's desire to offer this very difficult movement to the very best of his ability. With a horse that is naturally talented, the rider can often get away with less preparation and work to produce a good piaffe.

The piaffe is a movement I prefer to start teaching in a very loose and easy way, quite early on in the horse's career. I do this for several reasons, not the least because it is a very good exercise in helping to engage the horse, but also it then becomes just a part of normal work for the horse and so he doesn't think of it as anything

special; rather he will come to perform the piaffe in the same sort of way that one demands he perform the basic walk, trot and canter, in that he will offer the movement with plenty of enthusiasm, brightness and activity.

Whilst I may play a little with the shortened stride that will later lead to piaffe when I am long reining, I personally prefer to begin the piaffe when I am sitting on the horse. The way I like most to prepare him for this movement is to develop the simple transitions between walk and trot. When he will go brightly and lightly from a walk into an active trot by just a touch of my leg, possibly at this stage aided by a quiet click of the tongue or a very light tap of the whip, then the transition can be developed further to begin the first steps of the piaffe. I use my voice because I find it is a great way of not having to use a heavier and heavier physical aid. If a harsh leg and whip aid is constantly used, it will become embedded in his mind, and this will create a horse that at best will only piaffe under duress.

Gradually shorten the strides of the transition so that instead of the horse pushing forwards, he starts to push upwards. It is very important at this stage that the rider is extremely careful to make sure that the piaffe is working forwards up from the leg to the hand; in no way must the horse be pulled back in an attempt to shorten the stride. He should, however, be taught to step higher and more actively forwards. If you fail to teach the horse this way, at best you will have a shuffle on the spot that is totally dependent on how hard the rider can push the horse on, rather than the horse having its own desire to take the steps for the rider. If at any stage during the shortening of the stride the rider feels that the horse is getting a little lethargic, or lacking willingness in taking the strides, it is really important to go back to re-establishing the simple walk-to-trot transitions, so that once again they are achieved as very light, easy movements. If there is any requirement on the part of the rider to use a lot of physical strength either in the walk-to-trot transitions, or in the piaffe, then

things must be corrected at this stage or the performing of this movement will start to go seriously wrong.

Once the horse has the basic idea of what the piaffe requires from him, I then prefer to use a very gentle leg and click of the tongue to make him offer the movement to me, because I have found that once the horse learns to go off the voice, he will listen to a much lighter leg aid than if he is made to go off seat and leg alone. This will, however, depend on the horse's nature and his own sensitivity, rather than any magic tricks that the rider can do. Having said this, a good horse will be spoilt by being taught piaffe incorrectly; and bad horses often miss the chance of achieving the reasonable degree of ability necessary to do the piaffe, simply because the basic principles weren't adhered to.

When the horse is able to offer several strides with relative height and regularity, the rider can start to ask him to perform the piaffe with a little more cadence and even more height. However, it is important not to make the horse step too high, or too actively, too soon. If a horse has a natural tendency to take big steps, then this is all good and well, but the less extravagant horse should not be pushed too hard. The rider should be happy to accept light, shorter steps, as long as the rhythm and cadence is maintained, because in this way the horse will be able to perform the piaffe at a level which he is comfortable with, and in time, will allow the rider to push him more up to the bridle and thus gain more suspension in the stride. To try and develop the piaffe too quickly nearly always leads to a rather subservient movement.

So at this stage the piaffe should be a good, short, forward, springing movement. It shouldn't require too much effort from the horse, but it should require him to use his quarters even more. As his muscles develop and his self-carriage and strength increase, he should be able to perform the piaffe a little more on the spot and for longer periods of time. However, even in the first year or so of teaching the piaffe, it is quite normal to keep the strides quite short, but forward-moving, so that the horse may gain up to a metre of ground in several steps of piaffe. This is very useful for two reasons: firstly, it makes sure that the horse is always thinking upwards and forwards in the piaffe; and secondly, it is a very good preparatory stage for the passage.

(Page 126) Jennie Loriston-Clarke on Dutch Gold in piaffe
(Page 127) Ringmaster and Dane in piaffe
(Opposite) Obereiter Franz Rochowansky of the Spanish Riding School in an exemplary piaffe

PASSAGE

The passage is a highly elevated and collected trot. The horse should move forwards with a regular rhythm but with enhanced elasticity. The strides should be measured and pronounced with increased height and accentuated flexion of the knees and hocks. The carriage of the horse should be enhanced, with the hocks carrying a greater proportion of the weight. The contact should remain light, with the poll as the highest point.

Generally speaking, I prefer to develop the passage from the piaffe, although this is a subject most trainers will agree to disagree upon. It is something that is really rather dependent on the horse's own ability. The danger of allowing a horse to passage before he can piaffe is that he may not learn to sit enough behind, and therefore, whilst such a passage may look attractive and have plenty of height, it may not have the requirements of the classical system, and it can eventually lead to difficulties in teaching the horse the piaffe. The tendency in this case is for the horse to produce a piaffe that is both rather stiff-legged and croup high. Problems can also arise in doing the transitions from piaffe to passage and vice versa. Having said this, there will always be horses that have learned the passage first and will be perfectly happy to piaffe later on without experiencing any difficulties at all; but I think it is as well that the rider is aware of the problems that are associated with teaching the passage before the piaffe.

The way in which I favour teaching the passage is to develop the teaching of the piaffe, and then when this has plenty of swing, to push it gradually forwards and forwards until the horse starts to gain both confidence and a higher stride; then I introduce cadence by pushing him up into the passage. This method takes a little longer in the primary stages of training, although as in all schooling work, it is rather dependent on the talent of the individual horse. However, I find that in the long run, the horse learns very easily to come into the passage and piaffe, and so the transitions between the two movements become much smoother also.

Guadeloupe in passage prior to competing at the Catherston Grand Prix

Once the horse has the basic idea of the passage being a slower, more cadenced stride, depending on how he has taken to the work, then there are several techniques that can be used to create more height and lift in the passage itself. One of the simplest ways to enhance the passage strides is to push the horse from a very forwards piaffe-cum-passage, into a medium, or even extended trot, and then push the horse again up into the passage. The energy available to you in the trot should thereby be increased and then transferred up into the passage strides, and is often more effective than working too hard on just the passage itself.

Regarding all piaffe and passage training, it is best to work in short bursts rather than go on and on. Obviously this will depend on the nature and temperament of the horse, but short periods followed by a rest are usually the best way to teach horses most of the movements. It is important whilst doing the work in both the piaffe and passage that the basic way of going of the horse is maintained. It is probably well worth while breaking off from the more advanced work to ride the horse round and deep for five minutes or so, simply as a loosening technique and to make sure that the basic way of going is always reiterated. The rider should be checking that the basic rules of rhythm, obedience, forwardness and outline are always there. If all these principles are established, then the horse's self-carriage will be improved, and the piaffe and passage will also, as a consequence, improve.

In turn, the piaffe and passage, if performed correctly, will certainly improve the horse's carriage and way of going. As the horse progresses in his ability to perform piaffe and passage, so the sheer physical strength of his musculature will be improved, and this will enable him to use his physique to its maximum advantage.

Many people do like to use help from the ground by someone tapping the horse with a schooling whip, particularly for helping horses to get the idea of taking a bigger stride, and maybe even if the horse shows a tendency to be more lazy with one leg than with the other. In cases such as these, the schooling whip can obviously be useful as an aid, but it is something that should be used sparingly, because you can't take a schooling whip into the arena with you, so obviously the horse must learn to piaffe and passage independently of this whip. If it is used as an aid from the ground, the whip should be applied lightly and evenly around the horse's quarters. Exactly where it should be applied will depend on what the trainer is trying to achieve by using the whip, and on the horse's response to it. I find that most horses react better to repeated gentle flicks with maybe the odd sharp reminder, rather than the use of the whip in a harsh way.

It may also be of use to the trainer to revert sometimes to performing the piaffe and passage routine in hand. This can be done with the use of a single lunge line with the trainer walking alongside the horse, or possibly with the long reins, whereby the trainer works with the horse from behind. The reason these techniques can be of use is firstly, because the trainer is able to observe the movements of the horse clearly for himself from the ground; and it is also a good way to work the horse in piaffe and passage without the weight of the rider on his back, allowing him to get more comfortable without any disturbances from the rider.

Working the horse on long reins to improve the piaffe and passage is something I have also found very useful particularly in improving the transitions between these two movements. For a horse that might otherwise get a little fraught with the rider on his back, I find it quite easy actually to settle him down by working from the ground in this way. Naturally, it takes a fair degree of practice and tact before the rider or trainer can teach the horse in this way. And again, this method is really only an auxiliary aid in that the horse must be able to perform this movement under the rider. Nevertheless, it is a method that can be of great value with certain types of horses.

Finally, it is as well to remember in this discussion about the training of the piaffe and passage, that some horses just can't do it. At best they will offer some degree of what could be called piaffe or passage, but this will be their limit. As riders and trainers we must learn to recognise when our horse has reached his limit, because it is unfair to force him to attempt any movement that his natural physique makes it hard for him to perform. As the saying goes, 'You can't flog a dead horse!' However, you should not give up immediately every time you meet problems with any of the work, particularly with the piaffe and passage; some horses need more time than others to learn and consolidate what is being taught to them, and this period of time can vary from a few months to a few years.

PROBLEMS WITH PIROUETTES

• It is useful to remember that most of the problems encountered with pirouettes are caused not by the pirouette itself, but by the rider's approach to the pirouette and the horse's acceptance of the aids. If he is really listening to the rider and has a good understep with the hind legs, it is then a relatively easy task to turn him around in such a way that he performs the pirouette. But if the horse is behind the rider's leg, or against his hand, then this will be the main cause of the pirouette failing. More often than not, it will be a lack of enthusiasm in the canter that will be the cause of failure rather than over-enthusiasm. Either way, the rider must re-establish the horse's self-carriage and make sure that his strides are active and powerful, and that he is sufficiently forward thinking, before progressing further with the pirouette •

What if my horse loses the canter every time he approaches a pirouette?

This is a very common problem and one which is connected to the basic way of going, rather than with the actual pirouette itself. You can deal with this sort of problem in the following way by really pushing the horse up to the bridle and practising two particular exercises: first, canter on the spot, then move the horse on, then come back to cantering on the spot again, and repeat this exercise until the horse can maintain the canter stride. Secondly, if the horse tends to drop out of the canter stride very quickly then you must be more steady in your approach to collection; you probably need to take a few strides more than you would ideally want to, to make the horse fully collected. Try this, and just before you feel the horse begin to falter, then push him up into his 'normal' canter again. Once again, repeat this exercise until the horse finds it easy to maintain his collection in the canter.

Another useful approach to this particular problem is to push the horse up into collection, but then instead of doing a pirouette, ride a small circle of about 8–10 metres; when the horse can do this easily, the circle can be reduced to 6 metres. In this way he will get used to riding a small circle and being pushed up to the bridle, and once he can maintain the circle it is simply a matter of pushing him, in either shoulder-in or quarters-in, into the pirouette. I would suggest that the best way to lead your horse into the pirouette would be by doing two or three small circles, followed by a slightly tighter circle, rather than simply riding one circle and then the pirouette, as this will be of far less benefit to both rider and horse.

What if my horse throws himself sideways or dives round in the pirouette?

The circle technique explained for the foregoing problem is actually quite useful for this one also. If you use this approach, it is often a good idea to take the outside rein a little more firmly and wide to help hold the horse, whilst also holding him firmly with your legs, just to support him. If, as you are making the approach, the horse really starts to anticipate by moving sideways, then take him large and push him out onto either a straight line or a much bigger circle again until he learns to wait for you. You will need a little bit of a 'holding aid' to make the horse hesitate and wait for you, as the rider, rather than allowing him to use his own initiative and put the pirouette in as he wishes.

What if my horse loses his canter stride in the pirouette?

This is one of the more usual, but serious, faults to be seen in the canter pirouette. It is most important that the horse does actually maintain the canter stride during the pirouette; if he doesn't, it fails on one of its most basic principles. As well as the techniques we have discussed before, it is a very useful exercise to send the horse on into medium canter, bring him back to collected, and then send him on into medium again. This should be repeated several times until the horse is used to being pushed up into the bridle and significantly shortening his stride, but without losing the canter. What you must not do is perpetuate the problem by carrying on with the pirouette before the canter stride is re-established and the horse feels comfortable about maintaining it throughout the pirouette.

With this problem, it is important that the horse is totally responsive, particularly to the inside leg, so that the rider's pushing aids are really listened to. It is no use having the horse responsive only to the outside leg because all he will do is spin round and fall out of the canter when it suits him. The answer is therefore to make sure that the horse listens to both the leg aids, as well as the seat and the hand, so that he maintains the understep of the hind legs and produces a good pirouette.

Once this is established, it is wise to ride a fairly large pirouette to start with. The hind legs should describe a small circle of about 3–4 metres in diameter, and once the horse can maintain his canter in this size of pirouette, you can then ask him to describe an even smaller circle. However, any attempt to try to reduce the size of the circle before the horse can maintain the canter will simply lead to more problems.

What if I can collect my horse and keep the canter, but when I push him up into the pirouette, he is resistant on the turn?

This is a problem which may be caused by the horse's lack of response to the rider's aids. On the other hand, it may be that the horse has pushed his quarters in too far on the approach and therefore feels it is too difficult to draw his shoulders around his quarters. I find it most useful to push the horse into a very slightly exaggerated shoulder-in on the approach, and then to push the shoulder-in into a few strides of pirouette. In this way, the horse will have his shoulders well in advance of his quarters before he starts the pirouette. If the quarters are pushing in front of his shoulders, he will have a long way to travel round, and this is why he will often refuse to make the turn.

In the short term, it may also help to use a neck-reining technique with the outside rein. This must be done very cautiously, but it can be a useful way of pushing the shoulders round. The minute you feel a response, however, you should relax your aid and let the horse carry on and do the pirouette on his own.

PROBLEMS WITH PIAFFE AND PASSAGE

What if my horse becomes very tense when I begin this work with him?

Firstly, you must decide whether you have in fact reached a high enough stage in your horse's training to be able to introduce this kind of work to him. Some horses will pick up on the more difficult work at a very early age and as long as they are not stressed or strained in any way, there is no reason why they shouldn't be progressed quietly along the correct lines. However, some horses take much longer to settle at the basic work and then later, to become established in the more advanced work, seeming to need more time as much to gain their own confidence and strength, as to gain confidence in the rider. Some young horses can therefore really throw themselves into a panic when first asked to piaffe and passage.

Use your judgement as a rider to asses whether or not the horse is genuinely tense, or is simply being a little mischievous and using his tenseness as a way in which to evade the aids. If you are sure that he is being evasive, rather than inhibited by inability or panic, then it is necessary to push on and forwards. Otherwise I would suggest it is usually helpful to go back once again to the basic walk-to-trot transitions, and then to shorten the stride gradually whilst at the same time trying to create a little more energy – but being very cautious not to cause the horse to become too tense. A helpful analogy may be that you want to bring the horse to the boil, but you don't want him to boil over. To avoid this, back right off if he is threatening to become too upright. An inevitable part of training very tense horses will be teaching them to handle the pressures that go hand in hand with schooling and competition, and this can only be done with a lot of both patience and time. By all means take the horse to the edge of his capabilities, but not beyond the point where he will start to fight you. Also, be sure to reward the horse freely once he has given you all that he can, and then move on for five minutes and practise another exercise, before going back and asking for the piaffe/passage again.

Depending on how much the horse anticipates or worries, you have to decide how quickly or slowly you can forge ahead with your training of these movements. Most horses, once they are aware of what you require of them, do take to this work well, but to push a very sensitive horse too rapidly in respect of the piaffe and passage work at this level would really cause a great deal of damage to his overall confidence. Moreover it is not unusual, when you begin piaffe and passage, for the other paces to suffer, particularly the walk, and it is most important that the rider or trainer recognises when this is occurring and then takes the appropriate steps to re-establish the basics, before progressing with the more advanced training again.

Should a horse become really mischievous and threaten to run backwards or rear, it is extremely important that he is quickly ridden or driven forwards, so that he learns that he cannot nap out of this sort of work. Only when he accepts the forward aid can you then repeat the movement again.

What if my horse starts to swing from side to side, or plait his front legs in the piaffe or passage?
A horse that plaits its forelegs in the passage is often even more difficult to correct than a horse which does so in the piaffe. If this problem occurs in the piaffe, it is usually sufficient to push the horse more forwards until he gains more strength in his front legs, and then by gradually teaching him to come slowly back to piaffe on the spot, you will hopefully develop his hind legs until they get strong enough to carry the forelegs. However, if the horse's natural action is to plait its legs, then this problem will be much more difficult to correct, if not impossible, than if it were simply a training problem.

Sometimes careful assistance from the ground can help a horse maintain his impulsion in piaffe and passage. Dane helps Canadian rider Daphne Edwards-Haagmans on Voodoo

8

THE TEST
Preparing for the Competition and Riding the Test

When you start competing your horse or pony, it is very important first of all to decide the level of competition you are going to enter; in particular it should not be too difficult for either of you, especially if you have a young, inexperienced horse. It is sometimes a good idea just to take your horse along to a competition, possibly with a companion, so that he can get used to the atmosphere but without having the pressure of actually competing. Even the most placid of horses are likely to get quite excited the first couple times they go to a competition, if only because of the sheer number of other horses present at the showground.

It is often wise at this stage to begin by lungeing the horse at the competition, even though he may be perfectly placid at home. Ten or fifteen minutes of lungeing will usually be ample, as long as there is a suitable area in which to do it, and will help him to calm down and settle into his normal way of going. You can then work him for twenty minutes, half an hour or however long you feel you need to prepare him. It is sometimes a good idea to put him away then, particularly if you are at the show for the whole day, and take him out later in the day to work again. Don't fall into the trap of overworking your horse; just work quietly and calmly in a corner of the showground that allows you to concentrate and focus properly as you would if you were at home.

When you feel that your horse is ready to go to his first competition, be sure that the one you choose is well within your capabilities and those of your horse; for example, if your horse is able to do a Novice or Elementary test at home, it is probably wise to take him out at Preliminary level at the show. This rule is applicable throughout most of the horse's career, so even if you have trained him to Advanced level, if he has never been out before, it is probably wise to compete him at Medium level for the first few competitions. Always work well within your abilities and leave plenty in reserve so that the horse can shine in his test, rather than having to struggle through it.

It is also essential that you really acquaint yourself with the test you are going to ride, and the requirements of it. This does not necessarily mean that you must ride the test over and over at home, but that you ride enough of it – for example, several movements together – so the horse becomes accustomed to performing a sequence of movements; however, don't let him get to know the test too well, or he may start to anticipate it at the competition and it will lose 'sparkle' in performance. Even if you are having particular problems with a certain movement, it is still best to join it to another. Most tests have an overall requirement from the horse, and it is not just the

One of the most important things when riding a dressage test is to maintain a calm and relaxed state of mind

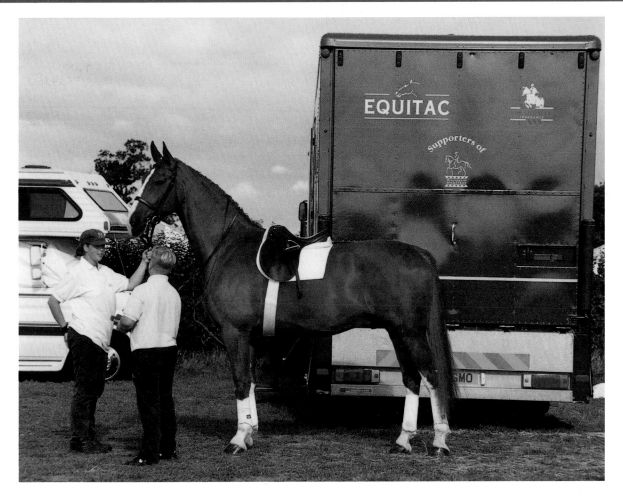

An immaculately turned-out Ringmaster about to compete at Hickstead in August 1994

individual circles, turns, or medium trot that gain the points, it is the horse's general way of going throughout the test. It is necessary, however, to have ridden the test through at least once at home, or maybe more if you are not a very experienced rider.

Make sure that you know the test more or less thoroughly, so that even if you are going to use a caller at the competition, you know what is coming next, and the caller is merely a prompt, rather than your only way of knowing what the next movement is. Arrive at the show in good time. It is helpful to have someone with you as an assistant; it is always easier to handle horses if you have someone on the ground and it saves you getting flustered. It is also much more fun to perform as part of a team than as

The half-pass in preparation for a Grand Prix test; the quarters are trailing slightly here as I am concentrating on making the horse go forwards as a priority. I will push the horse's quarters over more during the test

an individual. Turn your horse out well. If the weather is kind the day before, it may be an idea to give him a bath, or anyway wash his mane and tail. Make sure that he is well shod in plenty of time before you go to the show so you don't have any difficulty with his shoes once you get there; also make sure that all the tack is in good order, check that the stirrup leathers and reins are intact, and that there are no loose stitches. Numnahs and girths should be clean, and your own riding kit in good order, clean and tidy.

Most people plait their horses for shows. It is quite usual now to have the tail trimmed and the main plaited, and people will often use white tape in the mane to enhance the appearance of the plaits, although this is very much a matter of personal choice. Decide how much riding-in time your horse will need, and plan well ahead. Allow yourself at

Two smartly turned-out horses and riders, although they are not plaited up in this example

least a ten-minute margin for error, or the unthought of emergency that may arise. Try to avoid situations which would cause you or your horse to become tense or hassled: leave yourself plenty of time to tack up, mount, and make your way from the horse-box park or stables to the warm-up area, and enough time to actually warm up.

For young horses and inexperienced riders, the warm-up arena can often be quite an experience in itself; with so many horses in it, it is very often quite hard to find your own space to work. This is where the mental preparation of the rider is so important. You must not think of the warm-up as separate from the test: both warm-up and test should be considered as part of the same time period, and the warm-up time should lead naturally and progressively into the test. Furthermore, don't make the mistake of leaving all your best work in the warm-up area. It is very easy to show off a horse that is good in the extensions by riding them all the time, but at the expense of getting the overall picture settled. On the other hand, it is also important not to over-work your weak points: you can't train your horse in the warm-up arena – all your training should have been established at home. In fact the competition should be viewed as a test for your training, a pointer as to whether or not your horse is actually up to the standard that you thought he was.

Before you start warming up, you should have mentally planned the sort of time you want to spend on each movement. Usually it will take about ten to fifteen minutes to loosen the horse up properly; in this stage he should be worked calmly and fluently forwards in a nice round outline, in such a way that his muscles and limbs become thoroughly loose and supple, and so that any tension caused by the fact that he is at a show can be dispelled. You should then have a calm, easy horse to work with, as far as this is possible, for the next ten to fifteen minutes, and this should be used as a consolidation period. In this time you should actually start to perform some of the movements that you will be required to perform in the test. Again, don't pick on your weak points. If you have a horse that has a problem with the medium trot, simply take a little time to make sure that he is collected and fully engaged, rather than flying around trying to make him suddenly produce a medium trot that he can't produce at home anyway!

Think ahead, and keep looking up during the warm-up period; a lot of people are probably just as confused as you are, and if you don't, you might find yourself at risk of colliding with another horse. Having said this, mentally make your own space in the arena so that your thoughts are mainly on you and your horse, rather than everything else that is going on around you. If you are fortunate enough to have your trainer with you at the show, by all means concentrate on what he or she is saying as

well, but don't get over-focused on what other people around you are doing, because this will more than likely diminish your own performance.

I like to interrupt the warm-up work when I am at a show to give the horse the opportunity to walk more frequently than I would do at home, because I find that the tension that builds up at a show in some of the horses that I have is better dissipated by short periods of work, followed by short periods of rest. In this way, the horse creates a better feel for me as a rider and a better picture to the judge when he goes into the ring, without him having been simply forced into submission.

Make sure that your transitions are working well, and don't underestimate working on things like the halt. If you know you have a horse that anticipates the halt, work him forwards in a slightly more collected pace and then send him on without

Jennie and her entourage warming up prior to competing at Goodwood

British Dressage Supporters' Club judges' training day. Even judges have to be 'all-weather' nowadays!

practising the halt, only practising it maybe once before you enter the arena. A few kind words and a bit of encouragement are worth a lot more than using physical force.

Finally, after about half an hour to forty minutes' work, depending on the temperament of the horse, make sure you are ready to go into the arena in an alert, active state. If, as is often the case, you have to dress yourself, or remove boots from the horse, make sure that you do this at least ten minutes before you are due to go into the arena, so for the last ten minutes before you enter the ring you can focus clearly and concisely on the task that lies ahead of you.

Actually going in to ride your test is, once again, another mind game. There are many ways of describing it, but in one I imagine it as entering a rather convoluted pipe system: I would go into the pipe and concentrate. My mind must be thinking forwards, and only forwards, through the network of the pipe, rather than about what has gone on behind me. What I am really trying to illustrate by

this point is that you must close your mind against any other distraction when you enter the arena, thinking only of what you are currently doing, and what you have to do in the movements ahead; it is quite pointless to think or worry about anything that has gone on before, especially if you have made a few errors in the test. You really have to erase these thoughts from your mind and think only of the present moment and the next few minutes of the test. It is as well to remember that what has gone wrong can't be helped, but what you are going to do in the next few strides can be adjusted, preferably to your advantage. Always be thinking at least 30–40 metres ahead of yourself, so that you know what is coming next and so that you are planning clearly for the next few movements.

Above all when riding the test, just remember the basic rules of riding. The horse has to be obedient, but not subservient. He has to go forwards in such a way that he appears to be going forwards entirely of his own will; he has to maintain a regular and even rhythm, which must not falter throughout any of the work during the test. He must also maintain his self-carriage, so that at all times he is in balance and working with you as a rider. It is of no consequence if he performs a shoulder-in of exactly the right angle, if it lacks any of the basic principles that should enhance his way of going; thus it is much more important that he looks good and moves in an easy rhythm with a swing and cadence to his strides, than that he has exactly the right angle in the sideways movement. In other words, *the basics count the most*.

When you have finished riding your test, then that is the end of that session. Don't make the mistake of taking the horse outside the arena and starting to school him to correct an error that he may have made in the test. This is sometimes of use with certain highly strung horses, but in most cases it is purely a matter of the rider getting his own back on the horse for something he didn't do in the arena, and a practice such as this does not lead to either good horsemanship or good sportsmanship. If you have a problem that isn't quite working out, take the horse home and work on it there, and don't try and fix it on the showground. The dressage test is exactly what it says it is: a test of the stage of training you should

have achieved in your work at home.

Minor errors within the test should be overlooked. A young horse that is a bit skittish, or that shies in the odd corner should really be treated very lightly, and the problem should just be glossed over. If a horse is really mischievous and disobedient, it is probably worth taking him to many shows and riding several tests at each until he settles down.

When riding horses, you have to keep reminding yourself of the phrase 'I have time'. You do not want to waste this time, but you must move forwards without being rushed or hurried. In other words, make haste slowly! Enjoy your horse, the competition and the people around you. It is so easy, particularly in dressage, to get tied up mentally with the things that you know are going wrong, and as a consequence you stop enjoying the rest of the day, and fail to appreciate the things that have gone right.

Finished at last!

• *I have composed a short test, typical of those of Novice standard (approximately equivalent to AHSA First Level in the USA), to illustrate to the reader how the test should be ridden and what points the judges will be looking for. At Novice standard the rider should have established the correct position in the saddle, and the horse should be independent of the reins, free of stiffness and have a certain degree of self-carriage* •

A good start to a test. Victoria Simpson on Mester competing at Simon Fry's excellent show in Kent

A Enter at working trot.
X Halt, salute.   C Track right

A useful technique to practise when riding centre lines in the test is always to enter on the same rein that you intend to leave on. So, for example, the requirement of this test is for the rider to turn right at the end of the centre line: I would therefore advise that he also enters on the right rein, even if he has to come in from outside the arena. The horse will then be thinking right the whole way down the centre line, and will be less inclined to wander. Think also about the turn onto the centre line. At Novice level you can afford to make a half 10-metre circle turn from the side of the centre line. Make the turn smooth, and look to where you will be going to make sure that you are accurate.

Have plenty of impulsion down the centre line; more than you would usually think. If the horse is pushed forwards between the rider's hand and leg, he will be easier to steer and keep straight, and this again will prevent much of the wobbling that is often seen from novice horses on the centre line. Prepare well for your halt, keeping your legs on so that the horse stops straight and square.

Remember that your entry is the judges' first impression if you and your horse try to make it a good one, as the first impression is usually the one that lasts.

B Circle right 20 metres in working trot

Above all, it is important when riding circles in the test, to make sure that you are accurate. Think about the geometry of the circle before you enter the arena, so you are not thrown into sudden panic when faced with riding the movement. The

20-metre circle from B should touch a point 10 metres from X along the centre line. If the rider is aware of the required shape of the circle, he can then push forwards and steer accurately to create a smoothly rounded circle.

A Describe a three-looped serpentine ending at C

As with the riding of the circle, it is very important to ride the serpentine accurately and efficiently; serpentines occur in several Novice tests. Once again, think about how you will ride the movement before you enter the arena. Divide the arena into three equal parts and make sure that you ride straight across the centre of the school, so you are at right angles to the centre line when you cross it. If you get the dimensions correct, you should touch the track at the correct points and move crisply and cleanly away from it.

Make a clear difference between riding the loops and riding the corners. Ride deeply into the corner just before A. At A, technically, the serpentine begins and so the next corner should be ridden as part of the loop; at the top of the arena, ride the last turn around the corner before C as a loop, and then ride very clearly into the corner after C so that the judge can see clear differences. Remember, you can pick up marks on accuracy, even if your horse is not going very well, or being disobedient, so it is well worth while taking note of all the little details that can often count for so much.

M,X,K Change the rein showing a few lengthened strides

Firstly, you must think about riding the actual diagonal correctly before you can add the complication of riding the lengthened strides. Riding a diagonal is not just a matter of riding a straight line, but it includes the accurate riding of the all-important corners before and after it. By carefully choosing the size of the corner you want to turn, you can end up on the correct line across the diagonal, and polish it off by riding accurately and cleanly through the corner that follows it.

When you are on the short side, glance quickly at the marker you will be aiming to; in this case, K. This helps you to achieve a straight line on the diagonal and can enhance the smoothness of the turn from the corner onto your chosen line. On reaching the other side of the line, the rider is then free to change the horse's bend at will.

In the lengthened strides, the judge does not expect you to power across the diagonal. All that is expected is, as the test sheet says, a *few lengthened strides*. In the beginning, be progressive in asking your horse to lengthen, so that he is able to keep his balance and establish a good rhythm. The judge will be far happier to see a little lengthening, in which the horse maintains his self-carriage, than a hurried lengthening, in which the horse has been pushed too hard by the rider and consequently loses his balance and tempo.

B 20-metre circle left in working trot

Exactly the same principles apply here as in the 20-metre trot circle earlier on in the test; the only difference now is that you have changed the rein. A very novice horse may become a little unsettled by this, but just keep thinking and riding forwards, using your leg, your seat and your hands, in that order of preference, and remember to be accurate.

C Describe a three-looped serpentine ending at A

H,X,F Change the rein showing a few lengthened strides

A Medium walk. K,E,H Free walk on a long rein. H Medium walk

Make the transition from trot to walk smooth, and take plenty of time in preparing it. Once your horse is walking, establish a suitable rhythm, in which he is neither rushing, nor too slow. In the free walk, it is most important that the contact between your hands and the horse's mouth should be kept. In other words, do not throw away the reins – the test does not ask for walk on a *loose* rein. Ride through the corner with plenty of impulsion before the long side, and gently let out the reins so the horse stretches down his head to maintain the contact. Similarly, at the other end of the long side, take up the contact gently to re-establish the horse's head-carriage.

C Working trot. M Working canter right

Prepare your horse well for the upwards transitions. Make sure he is listening to your leg, so that when you ask him to move up into trot and then canter, it comes as no surprise.

M,B,F Working canter. A 20-metre circle right

Try to keep your horse as straight as

Collected canter – Grand Prix at Goodwood

possible down the long side, as the judges will be able to see all too well any crookedness. The same principles apply to the circle in canter as they did to that in trot; all that has changed is the pace you are travelling at, and therefore it is most likely that the speed has also altered. Simply think about establishing a beat that corresponds to the horse's rhythm so that you can correct any deviations smoothly.

K,X,M Change the rein. Give and retake the reins over X
The purpose of this exercise is to prove to the judge that your horse is in self-carriage, and that you are not supporting him with the reins. As you give the reins, the disturbance to his carriage and outline should be minimal. You only need to give the reins for about three or four strides, after which you can quietly retake them.

I find a useful trick here, is initially to give only the inside rein, that is, the one that the judges can see most clearly. In this way the horse will not suddenly feel totally abandoned and

will be less likely to rush off or to stick his head in the air. After a couple of strides, when you feel the horse has established his confidence, you can then give the outside rein as well.

M Working trot. C Working canter right and 20-metre circle
Once again, prepare the downward transition well so that your horse does not just fall in a heap at M. Make sure your horse is attentive for the canter transition, and be accurate with your circle.

H,X,F Change the rein. Give and retake the reins over X

A Down the centre line. X Halt and salute

In your pleasure at having nearly finished your test, or maybe in your haste to exit the arena, don't overlook the importance of this last centre line. Exactly the same principles apply as the entry. Ride plenty forwards enough, and when you have halted, salute and smile at the judge, before leaving the arena at a free walk on a long rein.

(Right) The end of the test

(Below) Sometimes it's all worthwhile! Jackie Bickley collects a prize at Hickstead

INDEX

Page numbers in *italics* indicate illustrations

Aids, 27, 29, 37, 52, 62
  acceptance of, 51
  order of priority, 56
  rein-back, 73
  repeated, 53
  transitions, 80
Attention, refocusing horse's, 27

Back, horse's, 51
Backward movement, *see* Rein-back
Badminton, 29, *61*
Balance
  improving, *see* Half-halt
  regaining, 81, 82
Bartels, Tineke, and Olympic
    Courage (Hol) in passage, *20*
Bend, 41, *86*
  maintaining, 63–4
  see also Overbend
Bickley, Jackie, *58, 59, 147*
Bredahl, Charlotte, with Monsieur
    (USA), *11*
'Bribery and corruption', *27*
Bridle
  double, 69–70, *69, 70*
  introduction to, 25
  snaffle 30, 69, *69*
Bridoon, 69, 70
Bright Spark, *see* Horsted Bright
    Spark
British Dressage Supporters' Club
    judges, *142*
British Young Riders Dressage
    Scheme team, *29*
Brushing boots, 31

Canter
  collected, *18–19*, 76, *76, 146*

described, 30, 102–3
extended, *62, 81*
half-pass in, 97
lateral, 84
moving into, 55–6
nearly on spot, 119
pirouette, *16–17*, 118, *119*, 124,
    124–5
rhythm, 30, 56
transition from walk, 56
working, 145–6
see also Counter-canter; 'Flip-
    flop'; Flying changes; Pirouette
Carriage, *see* Self-carriage
Centre lines, riding, 144, 147
Changing the rein, 59–60, 145,
146
Circles
  10m, *52, 54–5*
  20m, *63*, 144, 145–6
  quarters falling in on/out of, 63, *63*
  riding, *8–9*, 50–6, 144, 145–6
  varying the size of, 37, 56
  walking, 52–3
'Classical' movements, 67, 73,
    107, 118
Clonakilty Corn Dolly, *148*
Coaz, Dall'ora (Italy), 110
Collection, 67, *68*, 69, 77, *81*, 82
  epitome of, 118
Commands, 27
Competitions, *see* Tests and
    competitions
Confusion, 27
Contact, points of, 51
Controlling the horse, 24, 27
Corners, *64*
  consistently sized, 64–5
  maintaining speed before, 65
  negotiating, *50*, 59
Correction, 62
'Counter change of hand', 96
Counter-canter, 70–3, 76, 97

canter lost, 76
leg changes, 76
Counter-flexing, 57
Curb chain, 70

Danger, avoiding, 28, 31, 48
'Dialogue', 52, 58
Dikkiloo, *57, 94, 95*
Double bridle, 69–70, *69, 70*
Dressage
  aims, 30, 110
  for driving trials, *23*
  principles, 132, 142–3
Dutch Gold, *122, 126*

Edwards-Haagmans, Daphne
    (Can), *10–11, 135*
Engagement of hindquarters, 35,
    68, 77–8
Errors, riders', 80
Extended canter, *62, 81*
Extended trot, *12–13*, 14, *62*, 77,
    82–3, 125
  preparing for, *79*
  starting to teach, 82
Extension
  asking for, 81–2
  canter during, 98
  development, 81–3
  pace–quickening and running
      during, 98–9

FEI Prix St Georges, 72, 123
Flexibility, developing, 77–101
Flexion, 58, 59–60
  lateral, 33
'Flip-flop' changes, 109
Flying changes, *15*, 88, 102–17,
    110, 112
  aids ignored, 113–14
  arena locations, 107
  described, 102, 103
  earliness in front, 112–13

effecting, 103, 107
lateness behind, 111–13
lazy horse and, 112
one-tempi, 108–9
preparation for, 102
rushing away before, 117
set number of strides between,
    108
sideways tendency in, 116
tempi changes sequence broken,
    17
to left, *104–5*
to right, *104–5, 106*
two-, three-, and four-tempi, 108
'Four square', *61*
Freestyle tests, 110
Frustration of riders, 113
Fry, Simon: show, *144*

Going actively forwards, *32*
Goodwood, *27, 82–3, 122, 126,
    141, 146*
Grand Prix, 67
Grooming, 139, *140*
Guadeloupe, *82–3, 130–1*

Half-halt, *61*, 62, 66–7, 77
Half-pass, 44, 90, *94, 95, 96, 97,*
    138_
  in canter, 97
  and flying change, 107
  quarters leading and trailing, *99*
  teaching, 94–7
  zig-zag, 96
Half-pirouette, 118
Halt, 30
  square, 73 *see also* Half-halt
Hickstead, *139, 147*
Hindquarters, *see* Engagement
Holder, Alwyn, driving dressage,
    23
Hollowing, 65, *86*
Hoolahan, Sandra, *148*
Hooper, Frances, *60*
Hopscotch, *25*
Horsted Bright Spark, *26, 40–1,
    52, 54–5, 62, 68, 72, 80, 81, 88,
    92–3, 96, 104–5, 119*

Itis, *50*

Jogging, *see* Trot

Knife, use of, 48–9

Lahti, *110*
Lateral work
  aims, 84
  introducing, 84, 86, 88, 90
  principles, 93–4
  problems with, 99–101
Leg-yielding, 44, 84, 90
Legs
  clashing of, 100, 101
  plaiting of, 135
Lengthened strides, 145
Listening, encouragement of, 27
Long reining, 37, 39–41, *44*
  around school, 39–41, *40*
  changing the rein, 41, *42–3*
  equipment, *38–9, 39*
  safe, 40
  tangles, 49
  transition to, *36–7, 38, 39*
Loose rein, 51
Loriston-Clarke, Jennie, *29, 122,
    126, 141*
  Lizzie, *18–19, 22*
Lunge line, 30–2
Lunge roller, 31
Lunge whip, 31, *32–3, 35, 35, 45,
    45*, 48
Lunge whip, when ignored, 46
Lungeing, 30–7, *32–3, 34*
  changing rein, 36
  circle-shifting, 34
  falling inside circle, 34
  halt transition, 34
  hand position of trainer, 35–6
  problem-solving, 45–9, *45, 47*
  refusal to go forward, 46–7
  rushing from circle during, 46
  starting, 32–3
  tack, *31*
  as 'triangular' concept, 35
  turning inwards during, 45–6, *45*
  young/Advanced horses, 36–7

Mepham, Kirsty, *57, 94, 95*
Mester, *74, 75, 85, 86, 87, 89, 91,
    144*

Multiple changes, *see* Tempi
    changes

Napping, 46–7
Noseband, 69–70
Novice–standard test, 144–7

'One-two' changes, 109
Open rein, 51
Optimist, *57, 124–5*
Outline of horse, 58
Overbend, correcting, *74, 75*
Overtraining, 29, 109

Paces, problem-solving, 98–9
Park Royal, *60*
Partnership, horse/rider, 114, 116
  establishing, 24–9
Passage, 20, 81, 130, *130–1*, 132
  aptitude, 132
  defined, 130
  heightening, 132
  in hand, 132
  long-reining and, 44
  piaffe as preparation for, 128,
    130
  problem-solving, 134–5
Physical contact, points of, 51
Physical strength, 27, 29
Piaffe, 77, 78, 81, 125, *126, 127,
    128, 129*, 132
  aptitude, 132
  beginning the, 128
  defined, 125
  early teaching of, 125, 128
  heightening, 128
  in hand, 132
  long-reining and, 44
  problem-solving, 134–5
Pirouette, 88, 118–19, *119, 120–1,
    122, 123–4, 124–5*
  approaching the turn, 119, 123
  canter lost before, 133
  canter lost during, 133–4
  defined, 118
  leaving, 124
  motivation to perform, 123
  on spot, 124
  preparing for, 118–19
  problem-solving, 133–4

resistance on turn, 134
sideways motion, 133
to right, *120–1*
Plaiting, 139
Prix St Georges, 72, 123
Punishments, 47

Quarters, falling in or out, 99–100

Ramsier, Doris (Sui) on Renatus,
15
Rapport with horse, 24
Rawlins, Dane, *29, 57, 59, 79,
124–5, 127*
Rein-back, 44, 73–4, *74, 75*
crooked movement, 74
defined, 73
Reins
caught between legs, 41, 49
giving and retaking, 146
leaning on, 65
open, 51
tangled, 48–9
see also Changing the rein
Renvers, teaching, 92–3, *92–3*
Reprimands, 36, 47
Resistance, 100–1, *100, 101,
114–15*
Rhythm, 56
maintaining, *64*
Rider
interaction with horse, 114, 116
position of, 51, *51*
see also Partnership, horse/rider
Riding, starting, 50–2
Ringmaster, *127, 139*
Rochowansky, Franz, *129*
Rooster, The, *58, 59*
Rotterdam, *124–5*

Safety measures, 28, 31, 48
Salute, 147
Sanders-Keyzer, Anne-Marie (Hol)
on Amon, *21*
Schooling whip, 73, 132
Self-carriage, *75*
advancing, 66–78, *68*

in straight line, *58*
test of, 146
Senses used in influencing horses,
24
Serpentine loops, 107–8, 145
Shoulder-in, 65, 84, *85*, 86, *87*, 88,
89, 90, 97, *97*
angle, 86, *88*
development, 44
Shoulder-out, 84
Showjumping, 116
Side-reins, 31, 35
length, 47–8, *47*
resistance to, 48
use of, 48
Simpson, Victoria, *85, 89, 91, 144*
Snaffle, 30, 69, *69*
Stable, training in, 24, 25
Straight lines, 56–60
keeping, 65
Straightness, 57
Strides, lengthened, 145

Tangles, 48–9
Tecklenborg, Markus, on Franklin
(FRG), *16–17*
Temperaments, horses', 25
Tempi changes, 107–10
defined, 108
Tension, 24, 27
Tension, overcoming, 134–5
Tests and competitions, 123, 124,
136–47
Tests and competitions
acquaintance with, 137, 139
calm approach, *136–7*
choosing level, 137
mental attitude, 140–2
Novice standard, 144–7
preliminary exercises, 137
preparation: timetable, 139–40
skittishness at, 143
warm-up work, 140–2
Throughness, 59
Timson, Daniel, *52, 54–5, 80,
92–3, 96, 119*
Titbits, 28

Transitions, 60, 62, 77, 78, 79, 80
development, 77–8, 80–1
downward, 34
time span for, 78
to extended canter, 62
to extended trot, 62
upward, 80–1
Travers, teaching, 90, *90, 91*
Trot, 53
described, 30
extended, *see* Extended trot
forward-going, 53–4
lateral, 84
medium, *80*
rhythm, 30, 56
rising, 53
sitting, 53
transition from walk, 128
working, 145, 146–7
see also Piaffe
Trust, 50
Turn
preparing for, 57–8
see also Corners; Pirouette

Unresponsiveness, overcoming,
113–14
Unsettled horse, *33*

Virtu, *79*
Voice as aid, 28, 51, 73
Volte, 37, 59, 118
Voodoo, *10–11, 135*

Walk
medium, 145
rhythm, 30, 56
'Weight training', 78
Whips
for long reining, 39
lunge, 31, *32–3*, 35, *35*, 45, *45*,
48
schooling, 73, 132

'Zig-zag half-pass', 96

ACKNOWLEDGEMENTS

I would like to thank the following people who have helped in the making of this book in one way or another: Jim Bellman and Pat Corner for teaching me: Domini Morgan for getting me into this sport; my father for paying for it!; Victoria Simpson for the impossible task of transcribing the manuscript; Karen Ryecart and Kit Houghton for the photographs; my sponsors, Kim and Paul Millham; and Sue Hall of David & Charles for her tolerance!

DANE RAWLINS